LORD, HAVE
MURPHY!

LORD, HAVE MURPHY!

JOSEPH L. FELIX

THOMAS NELSON INC, PUBLISHERS
NASHVILLE   NEW YORK

All rights reserved under International and Pan-American Conventions. Published in Nashville, Tennessee, by Thomas Nelson Inc., Publishers and simultaneously in Don Mills, Ontario, by Thomas Nelson & Sons (Canada) Limited. Manufactured in the United States of America.

First Edition

Library of Congress Cataloging in Publication Data

Felix, Joseph L   1931-
  Lord, have Murphy.

  1. Meditations. I. Title.
BV4832.2.F44 1978   242'.4   78-17229
ISBN 0-8407-5662-3

Dedicated to Hilda, Joe, Ceil, Paul, Greg, John, Jerry, Terri, and Chris.

You have proved beyond the faintest doubt that all things do work together for good for those who love God—and one another.

Contents

LORD, HAVE MURPHY!

PREFACE

Wouldn't you know it?

I work for years on a book about Murphy's Law and then, just before it's ready to go to press, some smart aleck comes out with a book on the same subject. Why do things like that always happen to me?

If you've ever had questions and feelings like that, you may find some help in this book. It's a book about hardship and suffering. It's a book about complaining and enduring. It's a book about trusting.

I can't understand God's reasons for letting this other book be published just as I was getting this manuscript in its final condition. Nor do I understand why, after I had searched for a long time to find out who Murphy was, the author of this new book glibly announces he has found out.

But I do know that God is in control and that He has reasons for these things. And I am one hundred percent confident He will make it all work out for the best. This assurance has given me a fresh outlook on life. Ordinary setbacks do not frustrate me as they used to; I am calmer and happier.

I think I might be transmitting some of this new attitude to those around me. The other day my youngest son came home from his paper route and calmly described an incident he had experienced in one of his deliveries. It seems that one of his customers has a dog that recently has been trained to fetch things. Each time my son threw the paper on the front porch, the dog would run after it and bring it back to him. This kind of thing could go on endlessly and lead to much Murphyish frustration. But my son kept his cool. Nonchalantly, he carried the paper to the porch and desposited it between the storm door and the front door.

See, he's learning.

Whatever useful lessons my family might learn from me will be only token repayment of my debt of gratitude to them. My faith in God's loving power in our lives has been vitally nurtured by the experience of generating and caring for eight children. My wife's faithful dedication to our family has been a constant source of inspiration.

I also want to acknowledge the important contribution of three writers in shaping my outlook on life. C. S. Lewis, Keith Miller, and Merlin Carothers represent three very different perspectives of Christian living. Each has helped me greatly to be more aware of the working of God's hand in my life.

There are many other writers who have contributed to the insights I am trying to share here. Those who have read widely might recognize allusions to and rephrasings of some of these authors' works. I cannot possibly give due credit to all of them.

Lord, You know who they are. Even as they wrote the books that would help me know You better, You saw me giving birth to this book in order to pass this heritage on to others of Your children. Even as Hilda and I shared our marriage vows, You saw each of our children being conceived and knew they would bring us closer to You. And even as that other author began his Murphy book, you knew I would be apologizing for calling him a smart aleck.

CHAPTER 1

FIRST LAWS

If anything can go wrong, invariably it will.
—Murphy's First Law

You may have heard of Murphy's Law. It gets quoted every once in awhile by people who want to let you know they've been around. Maybe you've wondered who on earth this Murphy guy was. Many people have.

Recently I read eight additional laws allegedly set forth by this same inconspicuous legislator. I was irresistibly tempted—perhaps inspired?—to write this book. It seemed to me that a lively, thoughtful discussion of those things that inevitably go wrong might be appealing and helpful.

Obviously, Murphy's first law isn't very compatible with God's inspired Word. In Paul's letter to the Romans we read: "We know that in everything God works for good with those who love him . . ." (8:28).

But you understand what Murphy meant. You've had your share of those days when nothing goes right. Maybe you're struggling with the kids to get them to stop clowning long enough to begin dinner. At top volume you shout, "All right, let's say grace!"

"GRR-ACE," they respond in unison.

After several more attempts you manage to get them quiet. Reverently you bow your head and in your most solemn tone you say, "Let us play."

We all have days like that. You bite into your fortune cookie almost expecting to find a summons. You break a wishbone with your child and the top flies off, leaving you and the young one both holding short ends. You stand in front of the mail box, letter in hand, wondering why you mailed your gloves.

Tucked away in my files I found a newspaper clipping—probably from twenty years ago. A Sesser, Illinois man turned down three hundred dollars for his pointer dog. (In the 1950s, three hundred dollars was a lot.) The man gave an eleven-year-old boy a dollar to take the dog to the vet to be inoculated. On the way, the lad met a policeman and asked him, "How about having this dog shot for me?" When the man asked the policeman about his dog, the officer showed him where the animal was buried.

A toll collector on a Virginia turnpike was walking back to his booth with a cup of coffee. He stopped to let a car pass through. As he watched in amazement, the driver gave him a warm smile and dropped her quarter into his cup.

A nurse in a Chicago hospital was trying to ease the embarrassment of her patient, who had given birth in the hospital elevator. "Don't feel bad," the nurse said. "Two years ago a woman delivered a baby right out on the front lawn."

At this the woman began to cry profusely. "That was me!" she wailed.

Realizing how often things really do seem to go wrong, I wanted to find out all I could about who Murphy was and how his law originated. I began visiting libraries and checking every reference source in sight. Not a single encyclopedia contained a reference to Murphy's Law. None of the biographical dictionaries listed a Murphy that claimed to have encoded this legislation. I even found a book called *Whose What*. Surely here. . . . I found Morgan's Raiders, Morton's Fork, and Mother Carey's Chickens, but no Murphy's Law.

When I asked one librarian whether she had ever heard of Murphy's Law, she looked immediately skeptical. But when I quoted the law to her, she dismissed the matter as unworthy of her attention. "I don't like that law!" she scowled.

Love and Order

Well, dear lady, it's not exactly what I like to think of as the guiding principle of the universe, either. But even as I type this, Murphyish things happen. I put a fresh sheet of paper into the typewriter and click off a few lines of copy. Then I look at the page and discover that someone has set the machine to single space. I have to take the page out, set the typewriter on double space, and start again.

The truth is, though, that every one of those stupid things that happen to mess us up is one of those same things Paul says work together for good for those who love God. They would even work together for good for everybody, but some of us want no part of it.

It is important to recognize that these events we experience one at a time work *together*. Sometimes an event *I* encounter works together with one that happens to *someone else*. We can't possibly understand how the good result comes about. It's very complex to us, but infinitely simple to God.

We do have the firm assurance of God's Word that His Spirit is constantly at work. And, as we need it, He gives us an occasional manifestation of His providence and we can see some of the goodness of the results.

For several days after I gave up my active search for information on Murphy, references to Murphy's Law kept entering my life. During one day at the office, three people who did not know I was planning this book cited

15

Murphy to me. A few days later my daughter got on an elevator, pushed a button for a higher floor, and the elevator went down. The only other passenger on the elevator said (of course), "Just like Murphy's Law."

At the table that evening, my daughter was narrating the incident and mentioned the proposed book. My son, who had missed some earlier discussions, chimed in, "I didn't know you were writing a book like that. I have several pages of material on Murphy's Law."

And so I was led through hours of research in libraries only to find the best information on old Murphy right in my own house. Even with my son's help, though, I wasn't able to establish Murphy's identity.* Whoever he was, it seems to me he should have looked harder at the world around him. Murphy's first law contradicts everthing faith reveals to me as I study the world around me. I see love and order. I see goodness that endures despite our blindness and our willfulness.

Everyday Miracles

Consider for a moment that our planet Earth with all its mountains, rivers, valleys, and great cities teeming with millions of inhabitants, at this very moment is shooting through space at a velocity of 58,400 miles per hour. And yet a tiny baby slumbers in her cradle without the least disturbance. Faithfully, every twenty-four hours, the earth rotates on its axis. Once a year it revolves around the sun. Things seem to be working pretty well.

Our sun is 94 million miles away. Compared with other celestial bodies it is just a tiny speck. Scientists

---

*According to the other book about Murphy, Captain Ed Murphy was a development engineer for Wright Field Aircraft Lab. He formulated the famous law in 1949 as a reaction to a malfunctioning strap transducer.

Now if I can just find out what a strap transducer is.

tell us there are many stars more than sixty thousand times as luminous as our sun. And all these innumerable stars and solar systems move through space in perfect harmony. Yup. Everything out there is running smoothly.

Now zoom in a little closer. Drop some seeds in the ground and watch tiny shoots break through the brown earth. See them grow taller day by day, developing into healthy vegetables that bring us nutrition. Every particle of matter in the universe, from tiny grain of sand to soaring eagle to throbbing heart of man, echoes God's infinite power.

We take these wonders for granted. The sun comes up in the east and goes down in the west. So what? We make little of the fact that if it ceased to emit its warmth for a single minute, life on earth would end.

The ordinary wonders of life tend to escape our notice because they conform to our understanding of natural law. Oh, once in a while we might remember to give praise or thanks because spring always comes when it is most needed. But we leave most of the wonder around us to provide its own fanfare.

There's a story told of Dr. John Witherspoon, one of the signers of the Declaration of Independence, which shows his appreciation of God's care. A neighbor came to him one morning and asked him to join in giving thanks. He explained that his horse had gone out of control while he was driving and the buggy had been totally wrecked, but he had come away unharmed. Dr. Witherspoon responded that he had an even more re markable experience. "Hundreds of times," he said, "I've driven over that same road. Not once has my horse run away or my buggy been wrecked."

We take the everyday wonders for granted because we have natural explanations for them. And so, in His wondrous mercy, God occasionally hits us right between the eyes with a sign of His protection that is obvious even in our state of myopia. If we can't explain it we call it a miracle. For God it must be just another act of perfect love.

C. S. Lewis said, "Everything *is* connected with everything else; but not all things are connected by the short and straight roads we expected." In other words, it is our imperfect understanding of God's natural laws that makes events seem miraculous. But God uses even our imperfections to bring about good. He makes His loving care more obvious to us by an act that defies our understanding.

It must have been much the same with the miracles Christ worked in His lifetime on the earth. He changed water to wine at Cana to help His newlywed friends begin life together with deeply rooted faith. He cured the paralytic to help His skeptical critics believe He had the power to forgive sin. He fed five thousand people with five loaves and two fishes to intensify the faith of His apostles. And ours.

"And yet," wrote Ronald Knox, ". . . what is the feeding of five thousand compared with that patient process by which vast plains of wheat . . . make the slices of bread you forgot to say prayers over yesterday?"

Of all the illustrations of providence we find in Christ's life, the magnificent "blunder" of Calvary is surely the most astounding. God turned man's most horrendous deed—the crucifixion of His Son—into the means of salvation for all mankind!

Who's in Charge?

I am trying to say that we need a firm belief about who is in charge of this world. All things—bright and beautiful or dismal and sordid. And we need to let our conviction influence our thoughts, pervade our actions, and be reflected in our responses to life's events.

What a comfort it should be to know that everything that will ever happen to us is completely under the control of an all-loving God! He sees all the frustrations and apparent defeats of our lives. Through things that He wills or permits to happen, He brings good results from every occurrence. This realization is enough to make you breathe easily even when the announcer promises "the most apprehensive news coverage of all time."

Consider the woman who telephoned the department store to complain about distortion in the picture on her new TV set. "I'm watching Channel 7 right now," she said, "and the man has a very long face."

"Lady," said the salesman, "right now the news is on Channel 7, and if you had to report the things that are happening these days you'd have a long face too."

Let them happen. We have no real cause for worry or fear.

In all the threats of evil in our lives God works with perfect authority and infinite power. We have only to admit our own powerlessness and turn each situation over to Him.

When we allow ourselves to be upset by our circumstances we are forgetting that the battle is God's, not ours. We need to let go and entrust ourselves completely to His power.

Often our ability to open ourselves to God is hampered by things we possess. These may be material goods, relationships with others, or perhaps attitudes of complacency or self-sufficiency.

Then God's great act of merciful love may be to strip us of those things that keep us from Him. Recall the lines from Francis Thompson's "Hound of Heaven":

All which I took from thee I did but take,
Not for thy harms,
But just that thou might'st seek it in My arms.

We need to remind ourselves that this God who takes away our treasured possessions is, in fact, all-powerful, all-knowing, and all-loving. Twenty years ago, when that prized pointer was shot in Sesser, Illinois, He saw me using the incident in this book. He may have had many other, more important reasons for permitting that event to happen, but His knowledge of my action today is certain.

Twenty centuries ago, the all-powerful, all-knowing, all-loving God-man told us His first law: "You shall love the Lord your God with all your heart, and with all your soul, and with all your mind" (Matt. 22:37). God wants your *all* simply because you can be completely happy only on those terms.

But what a demanding first law! We must go in for the full treatment. We must yield ourselves completely to let the Holy Spirit transform us, taking away all that our own inclinations might have us be and turning us into what He wants us to become. It's a little like an egg becoming a robin. It may be a difficult transformation, but it's a lot easier than it would be for the egg to fly.

Goofing Up

Yes, from each of us God wants our complete heart, soul, and mind. We're really not used to that kind of demand. Even as we try to satisfy our most urgent needs we use only a small part of our resources. According to psychologist William James, even a genius seldom uses more than ten or twenty percent of his capacity.

It's a lot easier to hide behind ol' Murph. Proudly we wear the black-and-blue school colors of Hard Knocks U. We see all the silver linings in other people's clouds. We have so many troubles that if anything bad should happen today we couldn't worry about it for three weeks.

In many ways we behave like the child whose mother told him God was up in his room with him and he didn't have to be afraid. "Mom," he said, "*you* come up and stay with God. I'm coming downstairs."

God wants our all—for our sakes. He may not require us to give up everything we have, but we must be ready to. In one way or another He will let us endure the painful process of discovering our own complete emptiness.

Sometimes we look at our circumstances and it seems we have been standing forever in one painful spot. We may have been trying with all we have to practice the Christian virtues, only to meet with repeated failure. This is an opportunity to discover our real need for God and turn to Him with a strong commitment of faith. Until our complete bankruptcy becomes real to us, we find it difficult to look beyond the immediate situation and see God.

Obviously, some of the worst misfortunes of our lives are of our own doing. Endowed with free will, we are able to choose evil over good. Our reasoning power, weakened through sin, will sometimes err in identifying the right course of action. In diverse ways we fall into mistakes that represent possible causes of future regret.

Just as with the misfortunes we have no control over, God permits our mistakes and uses them to produce still greater good in our lives. When we realize this and turn to Him in our weakness, the potential harmfulness is taken from our poor actions as poison is taken from a snakebite.

Some of our mistakes are not willful. Maybe you've run into a series of things—as I did in one period of my life—like buses, telephone poles, and other cars. One woman was visiting an ancient Greek temple with a friend, and they wanted some pictures. As she was posing in front of some fallen pillars, she said, "Don't get the car in the picture. My husband will think I ran into the building."

Mistakes behind the wheel, like the countless other errors of our lives, may lead to good results. Often the greatest good is simply the humbling effect they have on us. We need to temper this impact, though, to avoid discouragement and harmful regret. When you make a left turn from the right lane, you're probably just a little careless, not really what that driver behind you called you.

It almost never pays to look back with regret on our mistakes. We waste valuable energy brooding over irrevocable yesterdays. The apostle Paul charged us to leave these things behind. Trusting God's grace enables us to benefit from our errors and see the positive side of our lack of success.

Thomas Edison said he tried twenty thousand unsuccessful experiments looking for a substitute for lead in the manufacture of storage batteries. Asked whether he wasn't discouraged by this waste of effort, Edison replied, "There's nothing wasted. I have discovered twenty thousand things that won't work."

Discovery or Invention

Edison's mention of discovery brings to mind an important relationship between *discovery* and *invention*.

We think of Edison as an inventor rather than a discoverer. Ben Franklin *discovered* electricity. Edison *invented* the incandescent light, the phonograph, and the carbon telephone transmitter. We see invention as a product of the workings of human intelligence. Discovery, on the other hand, results from what looks like an accident or a mistake.

22

But in archaic usage the two terms were synonymous, and this comes closer to how things really are. To
invent is merely to discover what God has placed in our
creative intelligence. Without inspiration from the
Source of all truth, no good or beneficial invention
would ever take place.

Similarly, Einstein, Newton, and Euclid were not
creators of mathematical order. They were dis-
coverers. They found the truth that was already there.

When we fail to recognize God's hand in all of this,
we risk grotesque distortion. Scientists begin to see
themselves as gods rather than as mere mortals. They
attempt to take unto themselves the functions of a god,
claiming the right to decide who has the right to life and
who has not, and even seeking to create human life in a
test tube.

Sometimes when we fly too high God permits us to be
brought very low. The trials He allows may seem completely unreasonable. A devout mother of six young
children is left a widow when her husband is shot trying
to help a fellow human being. An athlete of great promise is paralyzed by a "freak accident." Our fondest
hopes for a brighter tomorrow are dashed by unpredictable events beyond human control.

It makes no sense. The concept of an all-loving God
seems totally inconsistent with life's repeated
"tragedies." We are tempted to doubt or to try to
manipulate God by praying insistently for a miracle.

The way of faith at times like this is to lay open the
heart and say simply, "I trust You." We must bring
ourselves to tell God, "Even though what is happening
makes no sense to me, I believe in Your love and Your
promises."

With this faith commitment we transcend the human
situation that confronts us. We acknowledge that God
is infinitely superior to us in His knowledge and power.
Because He is above us, we must look up to see Him.

We look beyond the immediate events that confront us and turn to God with complete trust in His providence.

Our commitment of faith and trust in the face of misfortune, then, is ultimately an act of love. Believing God, we choose His Word and His goodness over our own wishes and desires.

Praise the Lord, Ah-choo!

The commitment we need to make when Murphy's first law seems to be working requires faith that surpasses understanding. Even though our reason doesn't comprehend, we trust the Lord. For whatever is happening to us we express our praise and thanksgiving. We do not do this with an eye to having things changed or achieving any other selfish results. We praise simply on the basis of total acceptance of what God has sent us, knowing He will bring good from it.

'Taint easy. Even with our best efforts, a complaint is likely to be our initial response. But if our deliberate choice turns us to praise and thanksgiving, the static of our grumbling will promptly give way to the new symphony.

Perhaps you've made it through December, January, and February without a sneeze. Then March comes in with all the beauty of spring, and you come down with a cold. When that first sign of cold misery strikes, reach for the treatment that has brought comfort to thousands of cold sufferers. Hold back your "Why does everything always happen to me?" and express your gratitude by saying, "Praise the Lord . . . ah-choo!"

Why is praising God so important? Primarily because it brings us to an admission of truth. We acknowledge that those things He sends into our lives are beneficial and that He will bring good results from the evil things that He merely *permits* to happen.

Beyond this, however, our offering of thanksgiving

affects our viewpoint and attitudes. Psychology has helped us understand the impact of attitudes on actions. When we open ourselves to Jesus Christ, His grace works to let us behave more positively, to be more self-acceptant and more supportive of others. Sometimes adverse physical conditions will disappear at the same time.

A few years ago I was a member in good standing of the Oh-My-Aching-Back Club. The pains were continuous and often severe. Remedies the doctor suggested had done nothing to relieve me. One day when I was shaving (and grumbling) I saw an unchristian Christian in the mirror. With great effort, I forced myself to say from the heart, "Thanks for these back pains, Lord, whatever their purpose in my life." *At that moment* I felt the pain actually draining from my body. I have had no serious or recurrent back pain since.

Frequently God gives us understanding once we have given Him our trust. But our faith commitment must come first. If we had to understand before we believed, our limited human reason would make heretics of us all.

And so our wondrous, all-loving Creator draws us to Himself ever so patiently. He reveals to us the workings of His hand so that we might come to know and love Him. We can begin to know God through many of His manifestations in creation. We can experience Him in love, truth, beauty, integrity—wherever His light illumines our world.

But none of us can ever believe in all of God. Our limited natures make it impossible for us to encompass infinity.

We start, then, where we are. We see God's love in the smile of an infant. We hear Him in a sonata or the song of a lark. We experience Him most fully in the love of fellow men and especially in the love of Christ, our Brother.

"You have not chosen me; I have chosen you," says

the risen Christ who walks beside me. He is the God-man whose real presence I have experienced. He loves me enough to take the full burden of my guilt on Himself so that I may know peace.

He asks only that I walk in His way, with a trusting heart. I'll let Him handle Murphy. And as I move along through my bungling life, He transforms my daily blunders into a resounding symphony of praise.

CHAPTER 2

UNEXPECTED COMPLICATIONS

Nothing is ever as simple as it first seems.
— Murphy's Second Law

The second edict from lawman Murphy grows directly out of the first. In fact, the same could be said about each of the laws we will consider in the chapters that follow. He has given us one big law to guide our expectations. And then, to make it clearer and more specific he has given us several additional laws that help us apply the big law to our messed-up lives.

And so it follows logically from the everything-goes-wrong generalization that we continually encounter complications we don't expect. Think about the Pennsylvania man who finally decided to get rid of the squirrel that had been chattering away for weeks in a dormer of his home. To smoke out the squirrel the man built a fire. You guessed it—his whole roof went up in flames.

Things do get complicated! Often we take on what looks like an easy task and then, after we have made our commitment, we begin to encounter many complications we hadn't anticipated. Maybe it's just that the job is harder than we expected. Maybe we find that certain things we hadn't counted on have to be done first. Or maybe our own errors cause things to become more difficult.

Some of us have trouble doing anything right. In 1972, a Czechoslovakian woman learned that her husband betrayed her. This distressed her so much she decided to commit suicide by leaping from a third-story window. Ironically, she landed on her husband and killed him instead.

Unexpected turns of events often raise challenges to our faith. Why does God let things go so backward? Why does He permit misfortune to show up so often in our lives? Why so much suffering, anguish, and misery? We join our questions to that of a little boy whose simple prayer was, "Dear God, what's a cold for?"

Standing at the Complaint Counter

Until we begin to truly rely on God, we continue to harbor bitterness in our hearts. Some people seem to spend all their waking hours at the complaint counter. Any amount of self-pity we allow ourselves will lead us to resentment or discontent when things don't go our way.

Without confidence in God we are prone to develop patterns of thought and action that keep us from productive living. Instead of progressing in emotional maturity, we become engulfed in feeling sorry for ourselves. The result is often devastating. We come to feel we are at the mercy of forces outside ourselves with the power to turn our dispositions upside down and let loose a torrent of misfortune into our lives. "You may be paranoid, but that doesn't mean they're not out to get you," goes the saying. We become easily discouraged, we feel very much alone, and we have great difficulty seeing the positive side of anything.

Here are some common laments of self-pitying Christians:

- "I can't possibly keep up with it all."
- "Nobody cares what happens to me."
- "People are no good."
- "Why bother to try?"
- "Nothing I do ever goes right."
- "I just can't take it any more."

Consider the youngster who said to the doctor, "My mother told me you brought me into this world. Okay, I want to go back."

When we have that stop-the-world-and-let-me-off feeling, we need to face our emotions honestly. We need to acknowledge our tendency to self-pity, look for the reasons behind our feelings, and turn the whole matter over to God with loving confidence.

Dealing objectively with our feelings is not easy. Our first attempts to be honest with ourselves will probably be unsuccessful. If we persevere, though, we will move toward increased maturity. More and more we will be able to handle frustrations in an adult manner and not continue to revert to our childhood reactions.

What's going on inside us is usually the key to why things have suddenly taken a turn for the worse. If we are successful in identifying what we are experiencing, we will probably be able to trace its origins and view the entire situation more realistically.

Often we find that a small hurt we don't want to face up to sets off our negative feelings. Once underway, these emotions gain momentum on their own. This is another reason for seeking basic causes of our misery. Once we isolate the real cause we will be better able to keep it from infecting the rest of our lives.

After we have faced our feelings and tried to identify their causes, we must turn the entire matter over to the lordship of Christ. This renunciation permits the worthless objects of our desires to drop away. We retain our longing for those things that are part of God's plan. In God's will all things assume their value and meaning and may be seen in their true light. When we really accept God's will, we look at everything about us—all our possessions, desires, and problems—in a new perspective.

Our Greek friend Socrates expressed a helpful bit of truth: "If all our misfortunes were laid in one pile from which everyone had to take an equal portion, most people would be content to take back their own and depart."

Of course! Each "misfortune" is especially tailored to our needs by our all-loving God!

Our Complex Complexes

Feelings of persecution are only one example of the increasing psychological difficulties people are experiencing today. Our world is troubled. Those of us who earn a living by helping people solve their personal difficulties should be having a heyday—if we didn't have so many problems of our own!

Personal conflicts are many and varied. We seem to encounter more and more people who are sure nobody understands them and who wouldn't want it to be otherwise. Many have trouble with those they live with. "My husband has a dual personality," one woman said ruefully, "and I don't like either one."

Why so much trouble? Well, my old Friday night buddies included a pharmacist whom we often jokingly accused of spreading bacteria to increase business volume. Similarly, you might think that the multitude of psychology books appearing on the market is more a cause than a symptom of our troubled times.

But we live such complex lives! It's much more difficult than ever before to keep adequate perspective. Some of us have low tolerance levels. We slip into apathy or restlessness almost as soon as we are thwarted. Or we find escape in a world of make-believe where daydreams relieve us of the complexity of everyday living. Still others of us become aggressive and take out our bad days on those around us.

Bad days—we all have them. For many of us February is the best month of the year because it brings fewer bad days than any other month. Bad days often fall on Monday, but it might seem more like Monday falls on us.

These bad days of ours can have a very positive side if we learn to handle them. Let's take them as a challenge to discover more truth about ourselves and to give ourselves more completely to serving others. They can help us understand the bad days others have and give us greater empathy for their struggles.

At the very least, we should avoid burdening others with our troubles. Half of the people around us aren't interested anyway. And the others are delighted that we got what was coming to us.

Simply God

In sharp contrast to our complex lives is God's perfect simplicity. Because our understanding is limited, almost everything we become involved in seems very complicated. We often feel more like rats in a maze than priceless human beings with an eternal destiny.

But God, who gives us our a-mazing lives, designs the many passageways so that they lead directly to Him. He alone can look down on the thruways and the blind alleys and guide us home.

Trusting in His loving-kindness is not simply relying on God to do what we want. In fact, every plan of ours must be subject to His will. We must be ready to renounce any and every goal of our own in order that God might achieve His purposes.

31

When our plans vary from what God knows to be best for us, we tend to cling tenaciously to ours because we cannot see where His will is leading us. But this is where trust comes in. We simply need to put Him first. His activity in our world must receive our priority. Trust and submission to Jesus Christ must replace dependence on our own efforts.

Let's try to realize that when something does not turn out as we want, God's providence is always providing a better solution and serving a more important purpose. He may be turning us away from a blind alley that we would have walked into in good faith. Or He may be testing our faith in order to strengthen it, removing imperfect attachments we may have to things for their own sake. Seen in this light, obstacles equal success. In fact, they serve the divine purpose better than our versions of success do.

A recent professional venture of mine is the Skill Development Center, a learning facility for helping young students improve their math and reading. When the idea of the Center first came to me, I imagined it would be a very popular program. We were offering a unique combination of tutoring, psychological services, and computer support.

In addition, I felt a very strong conviction that establishing the Center was what God wanted me to do. The details of the plan came to me very spontaneously, as inspired thoughts usually come to human minds. And there was a remarkable coming together of circumstances that made the timing right.

Still, the Lord blessed me with the foresight to predict that the kind of success we were to experience with the Center might be very different from what we had in mind. This has proved to be one of the few accurate predictions of my life. Despite numerous promotional efforts. I am losing money on the Center every day. But I am very happy about it all. In place of the prosperity we envisioned, many important personal changes are taking place in our lives as we follow trustingly where God is leading us.

Growth Opportunities

Relying on God's divine power changes everything. Every failure becomes an opportunity for growth. Our haunting anxiety leaves us. We are no longer troubled by constant fear of failure as we seek to reach our goals. In simplicity and with free spirit, we move forward with those tasks that we see as our duty. We give up worrying about stumbling blocks or potential frustration. We rely not on methods of our own choosing, but on the power of the Holy Spirit, in whom we place all our trust.

In other words, we put ourselves in the providential mainstream. By carrying out what presents itself to us as God's will, we ally ourselves with His plan for our lives. When we do encounter obstacles, we approach them patiently and confidently, no longer needing the assurance of immediate, visible results from our efforts. As we become more successful in carrying out every action with this spirit of self-surrender, we fit more and more naturally into God's design for us.

Acting in this spirit, we can be sure we are truly in His hands. We become instruments through which He carries out His work in the world. And we can be completely confident He will handle His instruments with tender loving care.

Then when the unexpected happens, we can deal with it—even when it drastically changes our lives.

Of course, letting go of the obsolete dreams of our childhood is not an easy task. The familiar ideas of the past have an appealing comfort. But setting aside this security opens the door to a dynamic, steadily improving adult view of life that puts us more sharply in touch with the will of God.

Among my boyhood dreams was the hope of becoming a writer. There is nothing as effective as a mounting assemblage of rejection slips in causing reassessment of that ambition, especially as offspring also begin to assemble. And so I moved into a career in education and psychology, where the Lord had much work for me to do. Not until I turned my childhood dream over to Him with childlike confidence did I succeed with writing.

We do, of course, need to set a direction for our lives, and this process should be a deliberate one. We consciously choose what appears to be God's way. Then, at various stages of our lives, we refine our purposes and goals by the decisions we make. These decisions distinguish more important from less important, worthwhile from frivolous, satisfying from empty. But each of our dreams and plans should be subject to change in order to follow where God leads us.

In Chapter 1 we considered the first law Christ has given to show us His Father's way. This first and greatest commandment, directing us to love Him with the totality of our beings, encompasses "the whole law and the prophets." It is a simple, clear expression of what is necessary for each of us if we are to realize the purpose for which we were created. If we were unhampered by human limitations, we would need no further commands. (That's how heaven will be.)

To aid us through our complex human lives, God has provided ten commandments. Each of these follows as directly from His first law as Murphy's edicts come from the everything-goes-wrong generalization. Christ reinforced this direct relationship for us: "If you love me, you will keep my commandments" (John 14:15).

Loving Carefully

But our love is much too careful. The demand to love God with the whole heart, soul, and mind is both difficult and disturbing. After all, we tell ourselves, we are limited creatures. We have limited capacities.

We satisfy ourselves, then, with loving with calculated earnestness. We love, not with the wholeness of what we are and do, but only with a part. We find it natural to love and worship God at church on Sunday, but we find it strange to love and worship Him with our work on Monday.

The universe is the Lord's. He wants to share its goodness with us. The goodness that is best for me today may bring an aching heart. Anxiety may trace a record on my brow. Reversal and frustration may challenge my peace of mind.

If I am willing—firmly and consistently willing—to rely on my Creator and Redeemer, I will see clearly that nothing ever happens, either rapturous or revolting, except by the directive or permissive will of Him who loves me with an everlasting love. I am His child and He is my Father. No good father hurts a child for the sake of hurt.

Realizing this, we can place our quest for happiness entirely in an effort to do God's will. Happiness becomes not a primary goal but a by-product. The standard for judging the outcome of our efforts changes from the tangible results we observe or the satisfaction we feel to the purity of our intention to carry out the will of God. When we are truly open to what He wants of us, nothing can mar the excellence of the decisions and choices we make or the acts we perform.

Notice the wondrous simplicity this viewpoint brings to our lives. For so long we have lived as divided beings. We have tended to house our religious convictions in one part of our beings and the routine of our daily lives in another. Our contacts with people, the way we work or play, our thoughts and words are seldom truly affected by what we believe. But when we open ourselves as completely as we can to the will of God, the complexity that stems from being preoccupied with ourselves gives way to the simplicity that looks only for God. Our major concerns are now taken care of, not as the most crucial aspects of our human existence but simply as important parts of God's design for our lives.

Bummers of Our Own

But what about all the mistakes we make? How do these work together for good? Why did God make us so fallible?

True, we all have many bummers of our own. Nobody likes to make mistakes and yet we do it all the time. It's embarrassing. It causes an uneasiness that reaches right down to our bones.

Not long ago I gathered up a stack of books and took them back to the library. Remembering to return books by their due dates has always been somewhat difficult for me. This time, though, I got them all back on time except one. The title of the one I forgot? *The Memory Book.*

In an effort to promote the use of ZIP codes, the post office used Bill Keane's "Little Jeffy" on trucks and billboards. The comic strip youngster appeared in a sleeper suit that was open down the front. "Don't forget to ZIP it," he reminded postal patrons. But when the postmaster general sent Mr. Keane a letter of gratitude and two souvenir copies of the poster, both mailings had the wrong ZIP code!

And so it goes. From the wife who baked an eighteen-inch pie because she couldn't get any shorter rhubarb, to the movers who saw the box marked "china" and sent it there, we all find ourselves up to our femurs in miscues.

And how we hate to get caught! From the first time

36

Mama detected us slipping our hand into the cookie jar to the more recent shock of seeing the highway patrolman in our rearview mirror, we have a strong revulsion for having our imperfections brought to light. Contemporary novelist Jessamyn West points out that it is easier to forgive other people for their mistakes than to forgive them for witnessing ours.

In the same way we try to hide many of our mistakes from ourselves. Generally we attempt to pass the blame or look the other way. It is never easy to learn from the mistakes we make; we keep making many of the same errors again and again. We find it extremely difficult to accept our susceptibility to error.

We need to step back and look at the matter more objectively. Mistake-making is part of everyone's everyday experiences. Someone pointed out that our mistakes do serve a purpose: Just think of all the pleasure our friends get from telling us about them!

We need to realize that every mistake we make is an opportunity for learning and personal growth. If we can face our imperfections and be open to constructive suggestions from others, we can use every error as a stepping stone to personal improvement. On the other hand, if we brood over our bummers we can come to the point where we're afraid to take action.

A corporate executive once gave this advice: "Make sure you generate a reasonable number of mistakes." That's good. With the assurance that God will use our mistakes to produce beneficial effects, we can dare to act even when error is inevitable.

Ignoring Detour Signs

There are many times when our deficiencies take the form of deliberate choices. We know the right course of action and yet we turn deliberately from God's way.

Anyone who seriously attempts to obey His orders

over a period of time is bound to encounter some failures. Eventually it may seem we have fallen back completely, perhaps to a lower level than we started from.

We never know how bad we are until we try very hard to be good. We never know how strong our evil impulses are until we try to resist them. How does one army find out the strength of another except by fighting against it? We must go on fighting.

Sin is a reversal of love. When we sin, we take something that represents God's love and turn it over to love of self. Even then, God uses our evil acts to produce greater good.

When we claim a good for our own, having removed it from where it belongs, we are saddled with it until we say we are sorry and give it back. Then guilt is turned into love, the offense against love is lost in the infinite mercy of God, and He turns our evil deed into an even greater good result.

All of human history has known only one person who never yielded to temptation. For the rest of us, to try to live virtuous lives is inevitably to fail. The only way to avoid failure is to give up our attempt to resist our evil inclinations, and this brings us to an even more horrendous end.

Where, then, is our hope? In Christ, of course. Because He never once yielded to temptation, He alone knows completely what temptation means. God forgives our sin through the merits of Christ, our crucified Redeemer.

Sometimes Calvary is completely baffling to us. We know that Jesus, God in human flesh, took our guilt upon Himself. But we wonder why, if God was prepared to let us off, He didn't just declare it. Why punish an innocent person? Why, above all, His own Son?

If you think of Christ's suffering as punishment or mere retribution for evil, His death seems pointless. But if you realize there was a debt to be paid, it makes sense that someone with assets should pay it for those who have nothing. We all have shared in His fullness.

Ups and Downs

On Calvary's hill there were three crosses. Two held the bodies of criminals. These were hung up to die in the common disgrace prescribed by law. On the third cross hung a Man who had been scourged and crowned; He was a bleeding mass of wounds from head to foot. To any passerby, this Man in the middle would surely seem the greatest criminal of the three. Only a person with faith could recognize Him as the all-perfect Creator of the universe.

The thief on the left sneered and snarled at the Man in the middle. With his dying breath he cursed and mocked his Maker. The thief on the right, however, saw his God beneath the blood and wounds, and with his plea for pardon he won paradise.

The difference between the two thieves is the difference between nearsightedness and clear vision. The stark tragedy of the thief on the left is his failure to see beyond appearances. He had an opportunity to gain heaven by acknowledging that the spiked hand reaching toward him was the hand of God. But he failed his vision test.

That same hand reaches constantly towards us. If we open ourselves to clear vision, we will see it as the loving hand it is. We will recognize the hand of God beneath the ugliness of the wounds.

Without vision, we will join the thief on the left in cursing our misfortunes. Or we will mock the God who allows hurt to enter our lives. Without vision, we will continue to slash at the bush because it has thorns, forgetting that it can also have roses!

Being *willing* to see is all that God asks of us. Still, we will have our periods of darkness. The God we serve will be hidden from our view. The trials and monotony of everyday living will weigh heavily upon us at times and the prayers we say may seem totally uninspired and lifeless. Even though we force ourselves to be faithful in our religious practices, our words will seem empty and we will experience no satisfaction or consolation.

At such times we need to renew our resolution to be constant in our pursuit of God's will. Our firm resolution to be faithful will, by its very tenacity, continue to develop new strength. We will be able to struggle effectively against the selfish longing that wants to take up the strength we need for God's service.

Then, suddenly, we find ourselves praying with gusto again. Our dialogue with God seems completely natural; the process occurs as spontaneously as breathing. Comfort from God's holy Word comes without seeking it.

Such variation is entirely normal for a Christian. We have a tendency to believe we are closer to God when we feel enthusiastic about praying and when we recognize progress in our spiritual lives. In reality, our dry periods may be more worthwhile than the "good times" in terms of drawing near to our Creator. More importantly, we need to be confident that God is with us at all times, regardless of our moods. Whether we are on a high mountain or in a deep valley, He uses our total experiences to lead us to spiritual maturity in Him.

Bangs and Pangs

We should not be dismayed, therefore, when an unexpected spiritual low comes our way. We can have confidence that today's suffering will fade in the joy of tomorrow. Since Christ's triumph over death, Easter forever follows Good Friday.

We accept suffering as it comes, then. We try to

express gratitude for our share in Christ's Passion. And we go on, faltering, trying to follow in His footsteps and stay open to God's will for us.

My personal struggle to remain open to God's design has been intense and painful. I have closed off many corners of my heart for myself. He who stands knocking will not break in and plunder. I must force the door open—a small crack will do—and invite Him to come in and help Himself.

In giving up anything that is dear to us the most difficult step is acknowledging to ourselves that we are asked to renounce it. When we make this acknowledgment we have taken the major step of breaking down the obstacle that has stood between God and us. All that remains is to clear away the rubbish.

To be honest with ourselves and admit the need to give up things, we must have a special kind of freedom. This freedom is based not on a resolution to resist the many attractions that try to capture our wills, but rather on the diminished appeal those things have for us as a result of rearranged values and priorities.

God also uses suffering to free us to love. Often pain and sorrow are given to us not so much to test our strength, but to bring us to that level of helplessness where God must come to our rescue. Our Creator knows how little strength we have. He brings us to an awareness of our own weaknesses so that we might turn to Him in love. When we seek refuge in God, we honor Him and find our own fulfillment.

The Need for Comfort

Turning to God fulfills man's universal need for comfort. The popularity of the Twenty-third Psalm, "The Lord is my shepherd," reflects the universal awareness of a need to rely on God. The Psalm acknowledges the

41

reality of pain and hurt in our world: "I walk through the valley of the shadow of death . . ." and yet, with God at my side, "I fear no evil."

The Christian who faces reality is aware that misfortune can and will occur. He might die of cancer, be killed in a plane crash, be compelled to endure poverty, or find his marriage unsuccessful. But whatever the difficulty, he finds consolation in the rod and staff of God.

We often overlook one key aspect of the comfort that comes with turning to God. In the eighth chapter of Paul's letter to the Romans, he points out that the sufferings of the present do not deserve to be compared with the glory to come. Faith brings a new perspective to all the misfortunes of life, and it increases our awareness that our real home is not an earthly one. We are reminded that all the sufferings of this life will pass in God's good time; the glory of eternity will reduce even the gravest suffering to pallid insignificance.

The true Christian does not search for ultimate security in this life. Rather, he sets his sights on an eternal destiny and trusts the Good Shepherd to lead him home.

CHAPTER 3

LET'S SEE THAT BUDGET AGAIN

Everything you decide to do costs more than first estimated.

—Murphy's Third Law

Did you ever read something you wrote years ago and think, "This is really bad!"? You find yourself wanting to deny authorship or feeling contempt for the person you used to be. The words and ideas seem so immature or out-of-date that you just can't accept the writing as your own.

Yesterday my dear wife Hilda was looking for something in one of our desk drawers and came across a journal I had kept twenty-five years ago. Wow!

I had read in writers' magazines of the value of keeping a journal. Many great literary figures used this approach to preserve insights and ideas that came to them until they could make use of them in their writing. Well, I'm afraid my insights and ideas weren't very usable.

Even more absurd was a financial record I had kept, which we found tucked in among the pages of the old journal. This document brought some real laughs. It's hard to believe the economic changes that have taken place in a quarter of a century. Back then, fourteen cents bought a quart of milk.

The economy of the world we live in has been altered beyond recognition. Someone has said that the most revolting reading matter you find in stores today is the

43

price tags. Inflation can spiral for only so long before it makes us all dizzy.

Murphy's third law speaks to this point. It says you can count on things costing more than you think they will. And even if you do count on this, they will still cost more than you count on. I heard a country-western song in which a forsaken young lady sings, "The only thing I can count on now is my fingers." Don't try that at the supermarket.

God's Incredible Economy

Despite these startling economic changes, the wages of sin remain the same. But so also does our inheritance as God's children. We have been promised unending fulfillment of all our needs if we will merely accept the trust fund Christ has banked for us out of the reach of moths, rust, and thieves. Our protection plan surpasses that provided for the lily and the sparrow, even though they never violate God's laws as we do. How generous His goodness is!

There is probably no area of human concern where a deep trust in the providence of God is as great a blessing as it is where money is concerned. In this chapter I want to share some of the things this trust has meant to me. Although it will certainly be obvious, I want to remind you that these are the thoughts and experiences of a Christian psychologist-educator, not an economist.

Back in my journal-keeping days I often used to wonder whether the money I was able to save would be adequate. That was like asking whether the water that drips from the bathroom faucet *after* it gets a new washer is enough to swim in. Even if upon graduation from college I had immediately become president of Procter and Gamble I couldn't have saved enough to finance our family of ten.

Praise God—my wondering wasn't worrying. As I grew up in Cincinnati, I was deeply imbued with the belief that the Lord who created Mr. Proctor and Mr. Gamble is truly the Provider.

Some people get hung up on this. They try to look into the future to make sure they have adequate provision. Some deprive themselves of the joy of giving life to as many children as they might like to have in order to make sure there will be enough money to educate them.

The heart of the problem is that gold dust gets in our eyes, and then we are blinded to things as they really are. We put too much faith in our own judgment. We attach too much importance to our own ability to take care of things.

Too often we lose sight of the source of the good things we have. Even Smokey, our family beagle, is smarter than this. Watch him follow Mother around the kitchen after a meal. He knows she'll be getting the scraps ready. If the family has done a good job of plate-cleaning, she may have to mix them in with something a dog food manufacturer has concocted from the hind quarter of an old glue-factory horse. But Smokey does know where his gifts are coming from.

Our gifts from God are many. Sometimes it helps just to start listing them. As we begin to realize what our Creator's infinite generosity does for us, we become more appreciative, more trusting, and more open to using His gifts as He wants us to.

Resources: Time Is Money

Of the countless blessings we receive, two of the most important and universal are time and money. How we use these resources is crucial; it reflects the values that guide our lives.

Most of us would benefit by taking time to inventory our attitudes toward these two things. For instance, if nearly all our time is invested in work for which we are paid, we may be placing too much value on material things. This is especially true if gainful occupation begins to interfere with human relationships, family life, or our relationship with God.

We will discuss the use of time in more detail in the next chapter. But realizing that "time is money" makes it clear that we can spend this important resource for worthy or unworthy ends, for selfish or altruistic purposes.

Another helpful approach is to examine our check stubs. How we spend our money will also tell us a great deal about our values.

Money is an extension of ourselves. It is a resource that can be used for good or for evil. I can use the money I have to promote the cause of injustice. I can use it to gratify my own selfish desires. Or I can let my money go in my place to help others, to feed them, or to clothe them. My money can go where I do not have the time or the skill to go. It can be another pair of hands to heal or another pair of feet to walk where Christ would walk.

We should be aware that we are merely stewards of our financial resources. In gratitude for being entrusted with the money we have, we recognize our responsibility to use it wisely. Because we do not consider ourselves owners (the ownership is God's), we strive for willingness to use all that we have in the way God would have us use it. It isn't important whether we are poor or affluent; it is only important that we can give a good accounting of our stewardship.

Clearly, then, money itself is not evil. It can be used creatively or destructively. Our attitudes toward material possessions are crucial, and Christ has told us what these attitudes should be.

Poor in Spirit

The world has long equated happiness with economic security and luxury. But a distinguished young Man once climbed a hill in Palestine and inverted this definition. To the group that followed Him and sought to share His unique insights, Christ defined happiness or blessedness as consisting of persecution, peacemaking, purity, justice, meekness, and mourning. But He started with the most incredible of all ingredients— poverty of spirit!

By Christ's definition, man's first step toward happiness must be the escape from enslavement to material things. The man who desires only to gain possession of material things loses his way on the road to salvation. If he is to find happiness he must be open to surrendering all things in a spirit of detachment. This approach to happiness runs directly contrary to many of the inclinations of our nature.

People cannot help wanting things, and our physical world surrounds us with many material things that appeal to us. But it isn't the wanting itself that causes problems. Rather, it's how we want and how we express our desires. We must strive to seek and appreciate material things in the way God wants us to, following His will and not our own. We must be generous and openhearted and carefree about success or failure. Our material needs and desires should not be the center of our lives. When they pass, we must not clutch vainly and desperately at them.

Too often we desire things for their own sake or for the self-satisfaction they bring us. We enjoy using the things God has created for us, but we lose our appreciation of them. Occasionally we need to remind ourselves that all things derive their beauty and attractiveness from God. Then we can open ourselves to use them in accordance with His will and be ready to part with them when He sees fit.

Persons who are poor in spirit avoid measuring the value of life by earthly possessions. They recognize material things as temporary. Their criteria for determining success are the eternal realities, the values and principles of life that do not fade away.

In this same spirit, we recognize our complete emptiness before God. We have nothing that is worthwhile except what He has given us. According to the principles of God's economy, poverty comes before richness and emptiness before filling. Acknowledging our spiritual poverty makes room for the Holy Spirit to enter our souls. Only when we admit we are poor can we be made rich. Only as we are willing to acknowledge what C.S. Lewis calls our "bottomless indigence" are we ready for God to fill us with all that is good for us. Our own goodness is nothing but filthy rags before God. We are absolutely dependent upon His provision.

Haves and Have-Nots

As we move toward this outlook, God relieves us of the burdens of greed, lust, and ambition. We find ourselves more ready to love those about us and to share generously what we have. Imagine what a different world this would be if all men began to move seriously in this direction. How peaceful and truly blessed it would be if poverty of spirit became as characteristic of humans as status-seeking is now! If only the "haves" would show compassion and willingness to share with the "have-nots."

In striving to make good use of all our resources, it is very important to think of the needs of others. We can use our time well by spending it in the service of others. We can visit the sick, comfort the afflicted, and give an understanding ear to anyone who needs a listener. Our money, too, must be used in the service of others.

Knowing how well a story can reinforce an important truth, Christ gave us the parable of the rich man and Lazarus. The rich man was a playboy who surrounded himself with the luxury of fine clothes and gourmet foods. He felt good about his wealth because he saw it as a sign that he was in the Lord's good favor. Meantime, down at the gate sat Lazarus, a poor beggar, waiting for a few crumbs from the sumptuous table of the rich man. The dogs did fairly well, but poor Lazarus remained hungry.

There are many well-fed dogs in our world. Shockingly, there are also many starving people. The gulf that separates the haves from the have-nots is widening. A small percentage of the world's population increasingly claims ownership of a large percentage of its resources and material goods. The poor fall deeper and deeper into debt, destitution, and despair.

Those of us who have enough to live comfortable lives often sentimentalize the hardship of others. We tell ourselves that poverty is a blessing and glamorize what it is like to have to do without the essentials of material existence.

But poverty that is not freely chosen is a great evil. Poor people are real persons, not just statistics. For the most part they find themselves caught in a vicious circle, a culture of poverty.

Right here in the United States millions of people suffer from hunger, malnutrition, inadequate housing, and insufficient clothing. But poverty is not only physical hardship; it is a miserable combination of problems to be constantly and concurrently endured. Poverty is lack of education, lack of opportunity, the existence of unsanitary living conditions. Poverty is experiencing a hopeless existence, being frightened, discouraged, and defeated.

It is the duty of every one of us to share what we have in order to feed the hungry, give drink to the thirsty, and clothe the naked. To fail in this obligation is to fail in fulfilling God's first law, the law of love.

For many of us, carrying out our obligation is difficult because the poor are invisible to us. While we enjoy the richness of our material blessings they sit by the gate, hunger gnawing at their stomachs. We don't see them.

We need to look. We need to get up from our luxurious tables and walk down to the gates. We need to try to understand not only the visible, material needs but also the spiritual and psychological needs that accompany a life of poverty.

But perhaps the reason you are sitting at the table is not to enjoy a sumptuous meal but to go over the budget one more time in the hope of understanding "where it all goes." Under the pressure of meeting last month's bills or making tuition payments, it is difficult to realize that others have still more urgent needs.

Some years ago, a gentleman walked into a federal office building and asked, "Is this the war-on-poverty headquarters?"

"Yes," was the reply.

"Good," he said. "I'm here to surrender."

As Christians, we can have complete confidence that God will supply all our needs. He has promised this. Our spirit of giving should never be dampened by concern for self-provision. Christ fed five thousand people with about as much food as your refrigerator holds after your son and his teen-age friends finish with it (well, maybe a *little* more). When the guests at the Cana wedding got thirsty and the wine ran out, he worked a miracle with the water that people are still talking about two thousand years later.

Let the Lord be your investment counselor. He will give you advice that contradicts Sylvia Porter, but you'll never go wrong in following it. The wealth you accumulate as you remove the shirt from your back to hand it to a shivering pauper will never suffer deflation.

Who's Really Rich?

Concern for the poor is hampered by a sense of urgency in providing for our own needs. We often become so absorbed in the financial goals we set for ourselves that we fail to recognize the true richness that comes with giving ourselves away.

The Murphy law that says everything costs more than we anticipate aggravates this problem. Just when we think we're going to make ends meet, things come apart at the middle. We step up to the cashier to pay for the meal our family has eaten, and we find that the after-dinner mint we really need is located in Denver. What the butcher charges for liver suggests he thinks you want it for a transplant. And toy prices are outrageous; the Six-Million-Dollar Man is just about there!

God understands. He wants us to use the good things of the earth. He wants us to be interested in earning a livelihood, paying off debts, and providing for a family. But through all this He wants us to trust.

Besides sharing what we have, we can help others by encouraging wholesome attitudes. We can help those around us to appreciate the good things in their lives and to realize that true richness is much more than a mere accumulation of material possessions.

Parents have a responsibility to cultivate in their children sensible Christian attitudes toward money. The parent who is constantly fretting over the rising cost of living is saying to his or her child that money is extremely important. On the other hand, the parent who spends time beholding the lilies of the field and the birds of the air passes on a heritage of Christian attitudes.

The story is told of a father who found his young son

lighting a cigarette with a ten-dollar bill. "Young man," the father exclaimed in dismay, "how many times do I have to tell you that smoking is bad for you!"

We have many indications that young people of today are being trapped by a high standard of living. Many grow up in luxury, with nearly every wish and whim satisfied. The result is often a lack of appreciation of the material blessings with which God enriches our lives.

As an educator, I have seen one clear indicator of this lack of appreciation—the condition of the lost-and-found departments in many schools. Nearly every kind of possession imaginable shows up in these departments, and there is often little attempt to reclaim the objects turned in. Many of our youths obviously have a very careless, nonchalant attitude toward money and valuable possessions.

A few summers ago our sons worked at their high school during the summer, clearing out vacated lockers. Literally hundreds of dollars worth of school supplies and equipment, as well as many other items, had been abandoned at the close of the school year. Even though students had been advised that things left behind would be confiscated, many obviously had little or no concern.

There is, of course, a positive side to this phenomenon. Perhaps in a truer sense than generations ago, today's youth have learned the value of a dollar: it's not much. We think often about the effect of inflation in eroding the dollar's buying power, but we do not talk enough about the effect the passing of time has on all material possessions.

We need to realize that even if we could take it with us it would still weigh us down. The transformed condition of our human nature as we pass to eternal life frees us from dependence on a material world. The objects that exist in time and space are no longer necessary, and any attachment to them must be removed before we can enjoy our eternal reward.

In this light, our efforts to balance our budgets take on a different perspective. Gone—or at least diminished—is the desire to insure that we have enough money to buy things for our own comfort or to maintain an unrealistic standard of living. Abated is the tension that comes from worrying whether there will be enough to go around. Instead, we are free to focus simply on making the best possible use of our financial resources.

Often we feel our responsibility to use resources well is satisfied if we contribute five, ten, or twenty percent to "religion" or charity. We need to focus more on the remaining eighty, ninety, or ninety-five percent. If we truly see ourselves as stewards of the possessions God has entrusted to us, we will recognize the importance of putting everything to good use.

Making It Stretch

There are many approaches to using money well or "making it stretch." One gentleman announced that his wife "was having plastic surgery. I'm cutting off her credit cards." A Beverly Hills woman waited until the bill collector came and then handed him the whole stack.

Three more realistic ways seem worthy of discussion. Let's consider some practical budgeting or financial planning techniques and some workable ways of saving (economizing and putting in reserve).

In your financial planning, start with the most obvious needs. Survey your life situation and translate what you see as needs into some basic *goals*. Make sure these goals are meaningful to everyone who depends upon you for financial support.

Consider your budget merely a framework within

which you tailor a spending plan to fit your unique goals. There's no magic formula; the real secret is discipline. You should set up a plan that you and your family believe has a chance of working, and then stick to it.

Your goals should include both short-term and long-term aspirations. You might be striving for a specific short-term goal like getting a car paid off in a designated time period, but you also need long-term goals like financing college or paying off the mortgage.

After your goals have been defined you need to establish priorities among them. At the very least, distinguish the goals you consider essential from those that represent less important, perhaps loftier, aspirations.

Then determine your visible expenses. Go back over checkbook stubs, receipts, bills, and other notations of payment made. Keep a record for a month or two until you get the clearest possible idea of where your money is going. Be sure to include seasonal items such as increased heating costs in the winter or yard maintenance in warmer months.

It is also necessary to estimate your *income*. If you work for a regular salary or wage, you should be able to estimate with reasonable accuracy what your take-home pay will be for a year. Add to this whatever supplementary income you have—interest on savings accounts, dividends on investments, overtime pay, and the like. Include only that income you are reasonably sure of.

By comparing the cost of achieving your goals with the money you expect to have available, you can set up a working plan. Be ready to revise as necessary, but don't change merely on the basis of whim.

Here are a few other hints for preparing your financial plan:

1. Use the minimum projections of income and

maximum projections of expenditures. You may find that a bonus you're hoping for doesn't come through or your estimate of inflation falls a little short.

2. Don't attempt to model your financial plan after your neighbors'. They may be trying to live beyond their own means.

3. Close the door on the mistakes of spending you have made in the past. This applies to your own as well as to those of other family members.

4. Avoid unrealistic resolutions. It's best not to count on dramatic changes in personal habits that might save money. Many financial plans have been scrapped for such lack of realism.

And Stretch . . .

A second approach to stretching financial resources is saving. We talk of "saving money" in two distinct senses. First let's consider ways of economizing; then we'll look at some tricks people use to put money aside for future use.

If you really want to economize, there's no more effective way than doing without the things you know in your heart you really don't need. Learning to do without is an important lesson for all of us.

Recently my sister-in-law and her teen-aged son went to visit relatives in Germany. After seeing pictures and listening to exciting narratives upon their return, one of our boys asked, "Why don't we ever go to Germany?"

"Heck," another son interjected, "we don't even have enough money to go to King's Island [an amusement park]."

Our kids are learning to do without. They don't always enjoy the lesson or take it graciously. "Karen's only doing without one new doll—I'm doing without three." And sometimes it's painful to Mom and Dad to hear them talking wistfully about the ten-speeds, the pool tables, and the color TVs their friends have. But if we can help them associate these economy measures with sharing food with starving people, it goes a little better.

Doing without things you don't need will also mean avoiding impulsive purchases. You'll weigh your buying decisions with some care, especially when a large sum of money is involved. I did finally acquiesce to getting a family car with air conditioning when we were told we would have to place a special order to get one without.

A second means of economizing is to shop for the best prices you can find on items of comparable quality. Of course, this can be carried to extremes by spending more on gasoline than you save by shopping around. But some amount of shopping around does pay off.

Occasionally you can find a real sale or a special purchase on a major item. Thrift shops, rummage sales, and garage sales offer great opportunities for saving. It may take a while to accept the fact that there is no shame in wearing secondhand clothes. It may also seem strange to push the department store elevator button for the bargain basement instead of for the ladies' wear. But you'll get used to it.

It's also a good idea to keep close rein on credit purchases and keep finance charges at a minimum. Some of us older consumers remember when we were concerned about *how much* was required to pay for something rather than *how long*. Now we invest in our elaborate stereo equipment with its high-frequency payments, seldom thinking about the insight of the child who said, "If you have a debt, in arrears is where you'll get it if you don't pay up." Paying cash is still a good idea.

Finally, look for money leaks in your budget—places where you can tighten up. One husband took great pride in the fact that he cured his wife of smoking. (How can you keep a cigarette habit without any money?) We can often make relatively painless changes in our lifestyles that will help us economize. In family life, the use that is made of mad money often leads to mad spouses.

And Stretch!

We also use the term "savings" to represent money we set aside for future use. Even people with limited incomes have devised various methods of achieving this. I'd like to share some of these with you.

One of the oldest and simplest tricks is to decide not to spend coins of a particular denomination. At the end of each day put all such coins into a jar or piggy bank and let them accumulate. Any time you have a little extra money, of course, you can fatten the kitty. You might even want to throw in all the coins you don't really need at the end of each day.

Occasionally you may receive some unexpected money or have access to a part of your income you are not accustomed to depending on. Maybe you have just made the last payment on a major appliance or an automobile. Perhaps you even received an inheritance. If you have enough willpower, this can be a perfect opportunity for savings. Salary increases, liberal insurance settlements, and income-tax returns can be set aside in the same way.

Other tricks have also proved helpful. Some people with substantial incomes make it a habit to carry only as much money as they are likely to need during the day. This keeps them from buying unimportant things and frees them to bank a certain amount regularly. A patterned savings plan will also be helpful, provided you have enough determination to stay with it. Or you may want to try a "hidden savings" approach in which you ignore a certain portion of the monthly balance in your checking account and then regularly transfer what you accumulate into savings.

Savings, of course, can also take the form of investments when we spend our money in a way that will bring worthwhile returns. As a father, I have been eager to provide a solid education for my children. Well-developed minds and trained wills are more important legacies than money. We can be certain that our investment in education won't be devalued by inflation. This applies not only to provision for formal classroom education but also to other enriching experiences.

In the same way, we save by spending as we invest in our homes. The truth of this statement goes far beyond the real-estate value. By providing a home that the children will think of as a safe place of love and sharing, we are investing in the future of precious human beings.

Being able to leave an estate to one's children is satisfying, but it isn't always a good thing for the recipients. A large inheritance can take away personal motivation for excellent job performance. A fortune that is passed from one generation to another can be misused more easily than well used. But money we spend to raise strong, resourceful, and God-fearing children is very wisely invested.

We need not worry about material possessions. As we trust in the Lord, unshaken by Murphy-ish surprises, He will see us through.

CHAPTER 4

TIME'S UP!

Every activity takes more time than you have.
—Murphy's Fourth Law

It's Christmastime as I write this. How providential!
There is no other season of the year when both
money and time seem to be in such short supply. As we
wind down to the last few days before Christmas we
often feel a sense of panic as we stack up our sales slips
and review the things we still have to buy.

Murphy's fourth law says that time, like money, is
never sufficient to cover our needs. Maybe you belong
to a Christmas savings plan; you conscientiously set
aside what would seem to be an adequate amount to
cover the gifts you intend to purchase. Then you find
that prices have escalated to such an extent that your
money runs out about halfway down the list.

It's much the same with time. This year you were
going to start your Christmas shopping early. In fact,
you distinctly remember that first gift you bought on the
Fourth of July. But the independent feeling you had
then is all gone now, and once again you are enslaved to
the inevitable pressure every Christmas season seems
to bring.

As you rush from store to store, tension swells inside
you. Waiting for service recalls the ad in a Mas-
sachusetts newspaper: "Your gift will be mono-

grammed while you wait all day Saturday from 9:00 A.M. to 5:30 P.M." Someone took an informal survey once and found that what most people want for Christmas is two more weeks to get ready for it.

What has become of the tranquility of that Bethlehem midnight when time gave way to eternity as hate gave way to love? The angelic lullaby that filled the skies on that first Christmas was a paraphrase of the commandments this newborn King was to give us. "Glory to God in the highest [*love the Lord your God with your whole heart, mind, and soul*], and on earth peace, among men with whom he is pleased [*love your neighbor as yourself*]" (Luke 2:14).

How desperately we need to recapture a view of time that recognizes its primary purpose as giving glory to God! Many things interfere with such clear vision. Our harried condition is far from being full of peace and goodwill. As we consider Murphy's fourth law, I would like to deal with some of the problems of time in the present, past, and future, and to offer a few suggestions for using this important resource well.

First, let's realize that not everyone finds time passing too swiftly. Those who grieve, suffer loneliness, or experience boredom find time painfully abundant. They long for a future when their misery will be relieved; they crave timelessness.

Most of us, though, wonder how the quicksand got in our hourglasses. We hit middle age prematurely and are caught off guard when it hits back.

World Enough

Whenever I find myself rushing from one place to another as if time were running out, I like to stop and ask why. I am reminded of a cartoon in which a bearded street-corner prophet holds a sign saying, "The end is near!'' A gentleman walks past briskly on his way to his favorite bar. As he goes by he asks, ''Do I have time for a quick one?''

As I was preparing to write this chapter, the phrase ''world enough, and time'' kept sounding in my memory. English literature had been one important focus of my graduate study twenty-five years ago. But now I had to get out the reference books to trace the echoing phrase to a seventeenth-century poet, Andrew Marvell. Tempus does indeed fugit!

As time flies it brings many changes. Marvell was writing to his ''coy mistress.'' His plea was for the enjoyment of pleasure before ''time's winged chariot'' carried them to eternity. He compared the sensuous beauty of the present to the barrenness of the grave.

Change is, in fact, an inevitable result of the passing of time. If we think of time as the duration of a reality, then as we move from the reality of the present moment to that of the next moment some change always takes place. Conversely, no change or motion *can* take place except with the passing of time.

Motion also requires space. Space is an interval of distance between two objects or within an object. All real objects (physical realities) have three dimensions: height, width, and depth. These dimensions limit the physical existence of the objects. The motion of these objects is limited by the height, width, and depth of the space that surrounds them.

As Marvell was so acutely aware, we are all limited in the space and time we have. Only God is unlimited or infinite. What Marvell did not realize is that our destiny is to be raised beyond space and time.

In moving through our finite space and time, we sometimes experience an intense desire to be free of these limitations. Our reaching out to conquer space in the second half of the twentieth century is symbolic of this quest. So also we are under constant pressure to find more time. We never seem to have enough to accomplish the things that need doing.

A novelty item that makes me chuckle every time I see it is a small wooden disc that bears the label TUIT. The other words printed on the disc explain that the owner can now take care of everything he was going to do when he got "a round tuit."

We have many things in our lives that we intend to take care of someday when we have a little more time. Often we are haunted by the feeling that time is slipping by us and we have not yet been able to get our lives into proper working order.

We need to remind ourselves that God is in control. In his economy of time, He is completely able to give us more time or less time according to our needs. He is also able to *know* our needs without danger of error.

What's the Rush?

Isn't it ironic that traffic moves slowest during rush hours? Perhaps you have allowed yourself half an hour to get to an important meeting. Under ordinary circumstances this would be enough time. But an accident has tied up the expressway just enough to get you involved in rush-hour traffic. Who says misery loves company?

Take yourself off your schedule and let God put you on His. Employ Him as your timekeeper. He will see to it that you get where He wants you at the time He wants you there. If you turn over your days and hours to Him, He will manage your time perfectly.

I have often been delayed in traffic at times when I thought I could least afford it. Occasionally I have had sufficient faith and trust to say something like, "Thank you, God, for this opportunity to remember You. I know You will get me where I have to go on time if this is really important." Invariably I have arrived at these engagements as early as necessary.

I never seem to have enough time when I go to the bank. I usually look over the patrons waiting in each of the lines and try to decide which window will provide the fastest service. In one line I spot a tired-looking secretary clutching a handful of deposit slips. In another there is a pudgy gentleman carrying a canvas bag. In a third stands a mother with savings account books for each of her ten kids.

Finally I spot the fourth line—only three customers, each holding the lone slip of paper that represents their reward for the last week or two of work. I get in line. Two of the patrons are processed quickly, but as the third steps to the window the telephone rings, and the teller settles back for a long chat. "Well," I tell myself, "you did it again, Felix."

How do I always manage to pick the wrong line? It just could be, I suppose, that this is the Lord's way of teaching me to wait. Instead of always playing the fastest-line game, maybe I need to learn to use my waiting time well.

We don't like to wait. Especially in this modern age, we don't like to take our time about doing things. We want to get finished with our jobs quickly. We are eager to rush through each task and get on with the next without spending much time thinking.

There are exceptions, of course. One painter (on an hourly rate) took an extra long time to paint the kitchen. When the owner of the house complained, the painter's response was: "What's the rush? Michelangelo took seven years to paint the Sistine Chapel's ceiling."

Trust God's Plan

Trust in God's divine schedule assures us there will always be time enough to do what God wants us to do. To believe otherwise is to find fault with God's perfect plan. Surely the almighty, all-present, eternal God provides adequate time for us to do everything that is important in our lives.

Suppose you have been trying to place a phone call for twenty minutes. First, you had to wait until you found the right threatening words to terminate your teen-age son's conversation. Then you dialed the wrong number. Maybe you got a busy signal or two. When you finally got through, the person you were calling had just left the house.

Perhaps your first temptation would be to rip the phone from the wall. But what kind of reponse would that be to this perfect moment God has planned for you? You can't possibly know why God chose not to have you make the contact. He may show you later. For now, just be glad He knows and is doing what is truly in your best interest. Try joking with your spouse or friend about it. Talking about it in the best possible humor may help you to be more acceptant.

One of the obstacles to really trusting that God is in command is our own lack of control. When we plan to accomplish a task within a specified time period and circumstances beyond our control prevent it, we conclude that we just don't have enough time. In reality, it may be that our estimate was inaccurate or that God really doesn't want us to do as we had planned in this instance. In either case we can be assured that His design is better than ours.

The sixteenth chapter of Acts tells the story of Paul's journey to Troas. This was not a trip Paul wanted to make. He had his heart set on going to Bithynia. He saw opportunity in Bithynia, Asia's richest province. Ending up in Troas was a real disappointment.

But Paul knew God had a purpose for his life. Even in this lowly place, he was sure he could find something worthwhile to do. Indeed, it was in Troas that Paul saw the vision of a man from Macedonia beckoning to him to come and help.

From Paul's example we can learn to trust God's control over events and circumstances. We need to cultivate the habit of seeing our disappointments as divine appointments.

The Ever-New Now

The specifics of your present moment comprise an assembled jigsaw puzzle of God's will for you. He has selected every single piece with care. Lovingly embrace the now God has put together for you. Accept the present moment with whatever task or pleasure, interruption or annoyance it brings.

Perhaps someone passes you on the street and pretends not to know you. God's will has permitted this to become part of your present. Maybe someone interrupts you in the middle of your Christmas budgeting or at some other time when you very much want to be alone. You receive a letter that is sharply critical of some action you have taken or something you have said. Rain interferes with a picnic you have planned. Someone puts you down with a scathing comment. Any of these pieces that God permits to be part of your present moment are indeed His will for you.

Now is an ambassador declaring the will of God for us and beckoning to our hearts to accept. As we bring ourselves to say "yes" to now and "thanks" for each moment fleeting past, we are turning ourselves over to God's care. There is no regret for the past and no worry for the future. No longer are others' acts of injustice or harshness a basis for distress or serious upset.

Although the difficult things can be received as the will of God, our Father also sends many more obvious blessings. He comforts us in prayer; He spares us grief that had seemed inevitable; He brings us to an unexpected success. A dear friend turns up after years of absence. The sun comes out after many days of gloom and rain. We receive an unexpected phone call with very happy news. Each of these good events invites us to open our hearts to God's will as reflected in the present moment.

Most of us need considerable practice to fully embrace each moment as it passes. Living fully in the present is not as easy as it sounds. Often we slip back into the old way. Some specter of a past encounter comes upon us or we face a difficult future situation, and our dedication to the present moment slips away from us.

At such a time we can only renounce again our regret or fear and turn the situation over to God. We need to take the focus of our attention off past and future and let our present thoughts, words, and deeds have the fullness of our human capacity.

In giving ourselves completely to the present moment we also give ourselves more fully to the people we are with at that time. Our relationships become more real and increase in their potential effectiveness. If you see me repeatedly looking at my watch and hear me voice concern about my next appointment, you will be less open with me than if you have my complete attention. My lack of concentration comes across to you as a lack of concern about you. On the other hand, if you see that I am trying to hear and understand what you are saying and doing, you will be better able to relate well with me.

Every moment that God gives us is loaded with infinite riches. We may partake of these in accordance with the extent of our faith and love. Because each moment contains God's will for us, nothing can add to or subtract from its infinite value. Each moment contains all that we can possibly desire.

Set this book aside for a moment and let yourself become fully absorbed in this moment. Don't wait until the kids are in bed or until the dishes are done; you'll postpone it further if you let yourself start putting it off. There is something in your life to be joyful about at this moment. Find it and appreciate it fully.

Nostalgic Knots

The other day I took a studied look at my baby girl. She has grown up.

Are there any feelings in the realm of human experience as mixed as those of a parent seeing his or her children reach maturity? Sure, we're glad to see them coming through the turmoil of youth without obvious signs of damaged personalities. Yes, we feel some sense of accomplishment that we have made adequate provision for their needs and weathered the recurring struggles that inevitably come with child-rearing. And there's some sense of relief. We sleep a little better (could it be sheer exhaustion?). We have more time to pursue our own interests. We seem to have less to worry about.

But what do I do about this nagging nostalgia? It keeps gripping at my throat and pushing tears through the ducts.

Vividly I recall the day some years ago when I watched this same little girl playing on the floor. She was in her early school years then. I watched her take from the cupboard her favorite punch-out display of Ice Capades characters and scenery and arrange them as she had many times before. With some forced enthusiasm, she began to move the cardboard skaters across the floor, trying to enjoy the colorful arrangement and make the characters come to life as they always had.

It didn't work. The magic was gone.

As we ourselves move toward maturity and then watch our own children grow, we are blessed with many touches of magic that are later to slip away.

Realizing they are gone sometimes brings overpowering sadness.

But even in those happy days when we always seemed to have children underfoot, I remember many moments of nostalgia. I would feel a touch of sadness when I stepped into a child's bedroom and watched him as he slept. So much joyful innocence was in his face. His look of peace seemed to fill the whole room with a wondrous calm. At such a time I would realize that a similar childlike peace was once mine, and I would feel some sorrow that this innocent happiness had slipped away with time.

Recalling happy experiences of the past is inevitable. All of us occasionally look back on the good old days when radios plugged in and toothbrushes didn't. Remembering isn't necessarily bad, no matter what emotional response it might evoke. To convert this natural human tendency to constructive use, however, sometimes requires a deliberate effort to be grateful. Instead of regretting the less satisfactory or less sentimentally satisfying conditions time's changes have brought, we must lift our hearts in thanksgiving to God for giving us the richness of these treasured moments.

After heaving that nostalgic sigh, we need to look beyond the here and now to that day of glory "when every tear will be wiped away." Then every good thing that has passed through our lives will be ours to enjoy more fully than we have ever been free to enjoy it in this life. Each of the happy experiences we wistfully recall will be ours again as part of the mosaic of eternity. Then we will directly experience the Source of all that is good in our lives. No joy we have ever known is really gone forever. Our Lord has merely taken it back into the treasury of His boundless goodness where we will discover it anew in our day of glory.

Sometimes when the happiest events of our lives have gone by, we feel a twinge of regret that we were not more open and ready to enjoy the pleasant experiences we have known. We had a party to celebrate some once-in-a-lifetime event, but the preparations tired us and attending to our guests distracted us from fully enjoying it. Our child speaks his first words or takes his first steps, but it is early in the morning and we are not fully awake. We find the one we want to love for a lifetime and we give our heart away, but somewhere in the back of our mind is the haunting doubt about whether this beautiful person is really the right one.

As we recapture these experiences in eternity, all the human difficulties that have impeded full enjoyment in this life will be lifted from us. Every neurosis, every fear, every uncertainty will be stripped away just as a traveler is relieved of a burden he has carried on a long journey.

Only One Regret

Many of us spend much time chewing the bitter cud of hindsight. We look at the past, counting the mistakes we have made and reminding ourselves of lost opportunities. We feel we have spoiled our lives or that our chance to be successful has escaped us. Our adult selves upbraid our juvenile selves for the foolish things we have done.

We need to push aside the roadblock of regret. Firmly, let's replace the words "if only" with "next time."

This is not to say that we should ignore our mistakes. If we do not acknowledge the times we have fallen short, we increase our chances of making the same mistakes over and over. But why are we so inclined to go over our past mistakes again and again? Basically, in recalling errors of our past or narrating disasters or disappointments of our lives, we keep ourselves at center stage. We remain the chief character in life's drama and satisfy our subconscious need for importance.

Our only regret about the past should be the creative kind of regret that permits us to acknowledge our human failings before God. Then we can remind ourselves of our utter inability to do what is right on our own. Relying on His support, we can point our lives in the direction of carrying out God's will for our futures and move forward with definite purposes. The more we stay in one place, lingering with our humiliation, failure, or sorrow, the more difficult it is to move on.

Someday time will be over for us; our earthly lives will be past. Then all that is precious in our lives—our work, our joy, our laughter, our prayers, everything but our sin—will be gathered together. All this will pass into the eternal now.

Who's Worrying?

Someone has defined a neurotic as one who worries about things that didn't happen in the past, rather than worrying about something that won't happen in the future, as normal people do.

There is a degree of normalcy in being concerned about what lies ahead of us. But often we try to look ahead into the darkness to discover things we really can never know. Too frequently we spoil the happiness of the present with imaginary fears about the future.

In recent years futurology has become popular. Alvin Toffler's best seller *Future Shock* has popularized the thesis that the rapid changes we are experiencing can paralyze us mentally and physically. Toffler notes the speed with which things pass through our experience, pointing out that modern man disposes of appliances, automobiles, and even homes with much the same ease as he does beer cans and ball-point pens.

Gone is the assurance that comes with being able to recognize familiar objects in order to locate ourselves in time and space. Gone also are the lifetime friendships people often experienced in a more stable society. The danger of loss of identity is critical.

But God's friendship endures. It remains beyond a lifetime—beyond *all* time. At any moment we choose we can pause briefly to recall His presence in us and regain our basic orientation as children of God. A moment spent in the presence of the unchanging Deity can help us find our bearings. We can renew our awareness of where we have come from and where we are going.

Psalm 37:5 instructs us to commit ourselves entirely to the Lord and rest assured that he will take action in our lives. We need to resolve to turn every moment of our lives over to Him, making at least a daily renewal of our trust and confidence.

Christ has taken away our reasons for being afraid. He has also removed the causes of our impatience for future time. Recognizing that His presence with us sanctifies this moment, we can wait patiently for Him to lead us in His way. We have no need to build dream castles; the divine Architect has designed for us mansions exceeding our wildest imagination.

What should this Christian realization mean in our daily lives? It should mean a fuller life-style. It should mean living in the present, making the most of each moment. It should mean abandoning the romantic recall or remorseful regret of the past and waiting patiently for whatever the future might bring.

The Gift of Time

One important aspect of carrying out God's will is performing the duties of whatever state of life He has placed us in. This is sometimes extremely challenging.

71

Our jobs become monotonous. It is difficult to go on day after day preparing meals for the family, being patient with rude and exacting customers, or settling down to serious study when the beauty of a summer day beckons us to be outdoors enjoying a game. Even when no cause is apparent we may find weariness pressing down upon us and giving us that tired-of-living feeling.

We need to follow our Lord's example in carrying out the ordinary, drab tasks of our lives. Christ's entire life was one long act of unwavering obedience to His Father's will. Of the thirty-three years assigned Him to spend on this earth, he spent thirty in the obscurity of his Nazareth home. The years of toil spent among the shavings and sawdust at His guardian's workbench might seem wasted. But through this drabness Christ carried out God's perfect will. He subjected Himself to the trivialities that surrounded Him with the same vigor He showed in preaching the Word of God to His disciples.

We'll discuss the Christian's attitude toward his job in a later chapter. For now, it is sufficient to emphasize that carrying out our day-to-day duties is one important aspect of making good use of the gift of time.

Another key emphasis in our attempt to use this resource well is focusing on the needs of others. To really live our lives for others, we need to make some specific commitments of our time on a gratuitous basis. Even if what we do is relatively small, we need to give some time to helping others without any kind of expected reward. We might seek to bring joy into the lives of the lonely by spending time reading or talking to them. We might go out of our way to help someone stranded along the highway. We might spend time preparing a meal for a family whose mother is sick. Rich or poor, we all have the resource of time to share with others who can benefit from our help.

TIME'S UP!

Using It Well

Business and industry have made sizable financial investments in time-conservation studies. This interest has led to some key insights that can be useful to anyone seeking to improve his use of time. I would like to share some of these ideas with you.

Generally, the most important requirement for improved use of time is a firm resolution to adopt whatever attitudes and systems might be necessary to accomplish this. Such determination will better equip you to tackle most difficult tasks promptly, rather than putting them off. It will also increase your ability to stay with a job until it is successfully completed. Setting deadlines for yourself will prove to be one of your most effective time-management techniques.

It is important, however, that you establish your own work rhythm. Some people accomplish most by plunging into each task and seeing it through to completion without taking a break. For others, the best way to accomplish difficult tasks, especially those involving the production of ideas, is to work on one problem until they start losing the feel of it and then turn to something else. Later they come back to the problem with fresh interest.

We need to develop an ability to filter out distractions or irrelevant activities. We need to find better ways of dealing with our tensions, be careful to get adequate rest, and make good use of our recreational time. Often a change in routine or the development of a new interest will be constructive. We can learn to conserve our energy by cutting down on our defensiveness and our criticism.

Take Time Out, Too

Effective time management can increase the amount of time we have to spend on leisure activities. We all

73

need some recreation. It keeps us from getting stale and refreshes us to do our jobs with more spirit. Even the hardworking ant takes time out to go on picnics.

Human beings today seem to have much difficulty enjoying free time. When we have time to spare we scurry around looking for things to do. Even when we force ourselves to take time out to sit and relax or engage in quiet social exchange, we usually don't enjoy it much.

One of the main causes of this phenomenon is the ideal image we have of ourselves: industrious and busy. We tend to equate greatness with productivity. If we see a young person enjoying idle relaxation or play, we are inclined to tell him to find something constructive to do. Similarly, we push ourselves to be continually engaged in activities that have a tangible product.

We need to cultivate Christ's ability to relax and enjoy His leisure time. In Mark 6:31 we see Jesus and His disciples setting out in their boats to withdraw to a quiet place on the shore. Jesus Himself called this time-out: "Come away by yourselves to a lonely place, and rest a while."

Christ also spent time relaxing with other friends. When he was near Bethany in the evening He would often visit the home of Martha, Mary, and Lazarus. In this quiet social atmosphere, He enjoyed their friendship as He ate with them.

In following our Master's example, we must stop judging the worthwhileness of our activity by its material results. The time we take for quiet relaxation will seem wasted if we look for measurable results, but recreation and rest are vital to our mental and physical health and serve to refresh us for a renewed commitment to God's service.

If visible accomplishments are not appropriate criteria for evaluating our leisure activities, how can we judge their value? First, we look for signs of God's will.

If one form of recreational activity that appeals to us is clearly contrary to God's law, we obviously need to turn toward more worthwhile use of our leisure. Is there someone with whom we should be sharing this spare time? If so, what would that person enjoy?

We should try to invest our leisure time with as much purity of heart as possible. This requires an occasional examination of our own motives. What are the things that influence us most in the decisions we make? Why did we choose to read this particular book? Why did we tell that funny story? When evidence of selfishness or other unworthy motives become apparent, we need to revise the bases upon which we choose our spare-time activities.

Take time out. Try to remember what it was like the first time you smelled a bonfire. Remember how the aroma of burning autumn leaves seemed to bring your sense of smell to a new aliveness! If we can re-awaken some of our ability to experience more fully the wonders of life, we will be richer and have more to give. We can know each moment of joy with fresh spontaneity. We can see again the beautiful dynamism of the world around us: constant growth and change to a new fullness of life and beauty.

Everything that comes into our lives appearing to be the end of something is the beginning of something else. Beyond every night there is a new dawn. The more we cultivate genuine trust in God's loving power, the more we are ready to put away the past and welcome the new experiences that await us *now*.

CHAPTER 5

HOW DID I GET INTO THIS?

It's easier to make a commitment or to get involved in something than it is to get out of it.
—Murphy's Fifth Law

Cincinnati is a great place to live. I've been here nearly all my life and I feel a sense of commitment to the city, its culture, and its educational system. Of all the other cities and towns I have visited, there is none I would rather raise my family in.

For some people, the city's many advantages can't compensate for the heat and humidity of its summers. Right now, though, the city is buried under fourteen inches of snow. Last night the official temperature was the lowest on record for the Queen City: 25 degrees below zero. We had been invited to dinner with friends. For awhile it seemed that the weather would force us to cancel, but the city's hardworking street maintenance crews promptly cleared the main roads. Since we had committed ourselves, it seemed reasonable to go ahead with our plans.

What we didn't know is that our friends were planning a cookout! If you've never tried to prepare a meal on the tundra, you can't really appreciate what it was like to stand calf-deep in snow and grill steaks in the record-breaking cold. Our commitments certainly do get us into some unusual situations!

Murphy's fifth law says we can't get out as easily as we get in. That's usually true. But I worry about the subtle implication: Getting out of things is desirable. I think it is usually good for us to stick with our commitments.

The idea of lasting commitment often seems outdated in our world of constant change. Some people consider it unreasonable for us to make permanent commitments to anything. A place to live, a vocation, a marriage partner, even a set of beliefs—all are seen as inevitably temporary.

We see such a rapid rate of geographic movement that it is indeed a rare human who remains in one locality for a lifetime. Friends come and go rather steadily and abiding relationships are unusual. People move from job to job and make numerous changes even in career fields. The deepest human commitment of all—that of husband and wife in marriage—has drastically decreased in its stability. As some down-home philosopher noted, it takes more and more horse sense and stable thinking to stay hitched.

In fact, lasting commitment is almost forbidden. For a dog to show lifelong loyalty to its master is admirable and worthy of praise. For humans to commit themselves in similar fashion is considered inconsistent with nature.

Need for Commitment

In the face of this transience, each of us needs to do some soul-searching concerning our outlook on commitment. Do we see commitment as a heavy weight imposed upon us, leaving us no freedom? Or do we see it as a simple matter of personal integrity, a matter of being truthful to ourselves? It is important that each of us be fundamentally faithful to ourselves. Only then will we be able to give ourselves to others without fear of rejection or lack of reciprocal commitment.

Uncommitted, self-centered living is the chief cause of the boredom that plagues our society. Without firm commitment, without lasting values, people are bound to experience emptiness. We all share in this problem.

We tend to take on a kind of reverse hypocrisy. Instead of pretending to be more than we are, we attempt to be less. We underaspire and refuse to commit ourselves to even the most basic causes.

Acting without commitment, we make important choices and decisions without firmness. Many people enter marriage before they have fully made up their minds. Someone wisely stated that people wouldn't get divorced for such trivial reasons if they didn't get married for such trivial reasons. Because they have not really and completely decided, they find themselves haunted by thoughts of possible happiness with someone else. Their indecision corrodes the foundation of their marriage contract.

We have within ourselves the power to make final decisions that bind us for life. To act in this way is not to surrender our freedom; rather, we are using our freedom to its greatest advantage. We are choosing to invest ourselves—all of ourselves—in a vocation, a marriage, or a style of life that we have judged worthy of our best efforts.

There is no better way to start growing than to put down roots. The growth that takes us from the self-centered immaturity of childhood to the emotional maturity required for love takes a personal commitment. The young child is totally tied up with his own needs. As his needs are met and he experiences love from others, he is gradually drawn outside himself to give attention to the welfare of others. Little by little, he learns to love.

In adolescence he encounters a period of continuing emotional growth. He enters the process of disengaging from his family. Many new growth possibilities present themselves in disjointed fashion. This time of awkward growth is important as a temporary developmental stage. Eventually, the emotionally healthy individual reaches a point where he or she is ready to make a permanent commitment.

Love is the only real justification for the permanent disposition of one's life. The needs and capacities people have can be fulfilled only through love. Attempts at permanent commitment that do not flow from love are apt to impede rather than foster continuing growth. At the same time, a commitment continuously impelled by love will necessarily have a quality of permanence.

Sticking Our Necks Out

Marriage has been compared to a violin—the strings are still attached after the beautiful music is over. In any marriage it is possible for the music to fade; commitment always involves some risk of regret. But we have to take the risk if we want to live fully.

"Lift up your eyes," the Lord counsels us, "and see how the fields are already white for harvest" (John 4:35). The world is beckoning more strongly than ever for today's Christian to become involved. The world is where life is lived, and life is the place where God and man may dwell together. Our faith must be interwoven with our daily way of life, and we must give ourselves wholeheartedly to every task our state of life demands of us.

We can find the fulfillment God wants us to enjoy in life only by the giving of ourselves. This is the only safe way to avoid the deadening effects of preoccupation with self. We need to change contemporary desperation to personal dedication.

It is by no means an exaggeration to say that each of us is irreplaceable in God's eyes. To you he has given a mission He has assigned to no one else. Immersing yourself totally in the way of life that lies before you—fulfilling His will—is your means of self-fulfillment.

The world is comprised of *doers, viewers,* and *yawners*. The doers are the few who make things happen; the viewers are those who sit back and watch; the yawners make up the overwhelming majority—they have no idea of what is taking place and couldn't care less.

Those who choose to be spectators, interested or not, are much to be pitied. John Henry Newman, a nineteenth-century Roman Catholic cardinal, said, "Fear not that your life shall come to an end, but rather that it shall never have a beginning."

A Seattle schoolteacher was standing in line at a grocery store when a man in front of her aimed a gun at the cashier. The woman kept her wits about her, took a bottle in hand, and calmly broke it over the gunman's head. Unfortunately he was a hardheaded thief and apparently was not even dazed. He kept his gun aimed at the cashier.

But a stockroom employee managed to put in a call to police while the store manager was opening the safe. The money had been neatly stacked and the gunman was preparing to make his getaway when police officers arrived and arrested him.

Sometimes when we take a chance and get involved, our efforts might not work out in the way we intend them to. Although we do need to assess the likelihood that we will accomplish what we set out to do, it is very easy to avoid taking action on the grounds that our small efforts will not make much difference.

We need to squander ourselves in living life fully.

God has provided us with everything we need for a full and happy life. However, He expects each of us to develop what He has given and discover our self-fulfillment in wholehearted living. We need to respond to the urge deep within us to venture forth into the deeper waters of life and take the risks that are necessary to accomplish worthwhile goals.

Struggling with Ourselves

We all have an innate drive toward adventure. We yearn to move from the shallow water out to deeper areas. But there is within us a lingering fear, because our way of life has roped off a safe wading area near the beach. Too often we continue splashing in the shallow water where we are secure. A precocious young student distinguished caution and cowardice this way: "Caution is when *you're* afraid and cowardice is when it's *somebody else*."

While one part of ourselves is urging us onward toward adventure, discovery, and progress, another instinctive drive impels us back toward security, stability, and repose. These two forces within us are in conflict. We are able to follow our instinct of adventure only as we repress the need for security. This conflict causes anxiety and stress. All of us experience this to some degree, but some find it completely disabling.

Much of the difficulty we have in making commitments is traceable to this internal struggle. I have counseled a number of people who, when faced with an important decision, were unable to act for a long time. They could not resolve the adventure/security conflict. Risk-taking was too threatening for them to deal with, and yet they were unable to accept the results of clinging to the safety of their present condition.

Unwillingness to risk commitment is one key problem, then. Its solution lies in a deep, abiding trust in

God. Whatever the risk, we can rest assured He will see us through.

None of us knows where our commitments will take us. We cannot (thank God!) know the future. Witness this notice in the London *Times:* "The Clairvoyant Society will not have its usual meeting this week, due to unforeseen circumstances." Only as we open ourselves to a wholehearted trust in God can we find the courage to make the commitments that will lead to happiness.

Overcommitment

There is another kind of problem that applies to some Christians. Sometimes we overcommit ourselves. We get involved in such a variety of activities that there just isn't enough of us to go around. Or perhaps we pursue a given commitment so completely that we narrow our range of self-giving and invest more of ourselves than we can justify. How does this come about?

Often our commitments spring from what Abraham Maslow has called our deficiency needs. We sense some important lack in our own personality or character and plunge ourselves into an activity or belief that offers hope of supplying this need. This kind of overcommitment results in a decrease of personal search, risk, and self-discovery.

Sometimes overcommitment is the result of weak faith. Perhaps we seek to derive from some person or object that which only God can provide. We set it up as an idol in place of God, who must always remain the prime object of our dedication.

Convictions and Stubbornness

I heard of a man in Coventry, England, who was always twenty minutes late. He refused to accept the

1922 time change, when clocks were moved ahead twenty minutes. "Nobody was going to take twenty minutes out of my life," he explained. "They won't beat me. I'm going to die twenty minutes late to show them I was right."

Now there's a man of conviction.

This resolute clinging to an unusual point of view might look more like stubbornness to you. Sometimes it's hard to draw the line. If we agree with the principle in question, we are apt to describe the person who is unwilling to compromise as a "person of conviction." On the other hand, if the principle seems unreasonable, we are inclined to apply the label "stubborn." And of course, there is a large area in between.

Now I don't really subscribe to the idea of keeping your watch twenty minutes behind the time everybody else is following. Our determined friend in Coventry was fired from a half-dozen jobs because of tardiness. But he probably got considerable satisfaction out of holding rigidly to his outlook, and he has certainly drawn attention to himself. Usually, though, resistance to change is self-defeating unless it is undergirded by lasting values or moral principles. A man or woman who still believes that God would have equipped us with wheels instead of feet if He wanted us to travel fast is likely to find survival in today's world something of a problem.

Let's not lose sight of the fact, though, that values are important, and we need people who will staunchly uphold them. Many of the values our society once held in high esteem have been abandoned today or sacrificed to the god of individuality. As a result, we find ourselves cut off from the authority that formerly shaped the character of our people. Formerly, the home, church, school, and community molded individuals according to the values they subscribed to. People developed an inner strength from those relationships, a feeling of belonging and responsibility. They respected loyalty, duty, and patriotism.

Today, however, the overriding concern is often a highly individualized self-interest. There is a strong demand for each person to be freed of familiar disciplines and externally imposed values.

Human Progress

One of the factors that has caused this change from institutional to individual emphasis is our growing appreciation for what the individual human being is capable of. We have been increasingly able to control heat, light, and other forms of energy. We have displayed mastery over plants and animals. We have gained a position of control over our own minds and bodies.

No longer, then, do we see ourselves fulfilling our roles simply by conforming to the order of nature and society. The traditional view that this order has been established by God for us to follow has now been replaced by a view that man must work out his own humanity. Since we are capable of mastering the world in the interest of progress, we now consider ourselves responsible for our own humanization.

There is a strong, positive element in this change. Readiness to question traditional beliefs can bring us to a healthy state of intellectual scrutiny. This is a marked improvement over blind acceptance of viewpoints passed on from former generations. Attempts to improve the status quo are desirable. Each step forward is achieved through courage, vision, and an adventurous spirit. Only through individual rebellion against unfortunate conditions and traditions that have outlived their usefulness are we led to a better way of life.

But we must maintain some balance. We must preserve the good while eliminating the bad, and this requires a willingness on our part to remain open to reasonable, defensible truths and values that demand something of us.

Nothing in this life is static. The universe is in a constant state of flux. Change is the very essence of time; only eternity will fix things in an unchanging condition. We know that even as we see things that appear to be unchanging, imperceptible changes are taking place. So also in our spiritual development there is constant change; either we are moving forward or we are regressing. Either we are working out the problems that interfere with our spiritual growth or these same problems are causing us to slip farther from our goals.

The Price of Growth

Christian growth is not without its price. We often get the impression that turning our lives over to Christ will somehow make them automatically exciting, consistent, and totally moral. We find, instead, that we continue to have times of doubt, boredom, and behavior inconsistent with our commitment. Along with spiritual growth comes a continuing struggle to overcome the downward pull of our human natures.

Among the things I remember most vividly about my childhood is the way my mother diagnosed almost every ache or pain I ever complained about. Whenever I would come to her with a sad tale about an aching muscle or a sore spot somewhere on my body, she would listen to what I had to say, give me a sympathetic look, and then proclaim, "It's just a growing pain."

No growth ever takes place without some pain. This axiom applies to spiritual as well as physical growth. If we are to move toward being the kind of persons God wants us to be, we must first be stripped of our old selves with their undesirable habits. Leaving behind what we were is painful. It requires that we entrust ourselves to God's care as He takes us forward into unexplored territory. Fear of the unknown threatens us. The possibility of having to survive in a wasteland brings fear to our souls, and yet we know the land toward which we journey flows with milk and honey. Becoming the persons God wants us to be means following the trail to happiness He has laid out for us.

It's crucial that we realize conversion to Christ brings freedom, not slavery. Only those who have died and live again in Christ are truly free. To give ourselves to God is the only real means of achieving the freedom for which we were created.

We are often inclined to shrink from a closer relationship with God because we fear that "having Him we have naught else besides." But God is not a joyless God who seeks to deprive us of things we treasure. He sent His Son to us to direct our hearts, not to destroy them. Christ came to lead us to a share in His life—the greatest richness man can know. It is the crowning of all other joys.

Transformation

All the faculties of our nature are raised up when we give them over to God. Distorted and cramped when used to serve ourselves, the forces of our hearts and minds begin to function in the dimension of grace when we permit them to be converted to God's service. A new principle of activity invades our lives and brings supernatural value to our works.

Any human faculty that is put to the use for which it was created will find fruition and peace. When our faculties are directed toward God, there will be order and harmony in our lives.

Thus, spiritual life is not a matter of mortification and death but rather of birth. Man's heart and will may be denied, but they can never be crushed. When we realize that these faculties have been created to be essentially

God-centered, we can begin to appreciate the transformation that takes place when we give ourselves to God

One Christmas when I was a boy, I received a baseball game. It was the kind in which you move the players around the bases on a board and roll dice to determine the pitches and hits. I must have spent more time playing that game than pulling weeds in the yard (and it seemed like pulling weeds was just about all I ever did). I played the game so much that I memorized the plays that went with different numbers on the dice.

We would use the phone book and other reference sources to make up names for players on our teams. Back then it didn't make much difference that these players had no identity beyond our own imagination. Bob Donovan was as real an outfielder as Joe Dimaggio as far as I was concerned. And how we identified with those players! We picked the people we wanted to be. Dad chose Cy Creighton, one of the finest catchers in the league.

But baseball players didn't last forever. I remember going to Dad one day when he was shaving and saying, "Dad, your guy died. Who do you want to be now?"

Dad came up with the name Labini Lazarini Lamink. Well, I wasn't about to write all that every time I made up my lineup. So my roster carried a shortstop called Lab Laz. Laz didn't last long.

A few years ago I introduced this baseball game to my sons. For the past several seasons we have all had teams (one of our best means of spending time together). In fact, the game has spread around our neighborhood to such an extent that one group of my son's friends had a league that played a full season of around two hundred games.

The Joy of Pretending

Now what does all this add up to? Obviously, it's fun to pretend. While the Felixes and their friends were giving imaginary life to baseball players, many young girls around the world were dressing up. By putting on their mothers' clothes or other things that didn't fit, these girls magically became television stars, princesses, or—better yet—mothers.

In all this pretending, children are reaching out to become something they are not. Dice in hand, my son suddenly becomes the best curve-ball pitcher in the league. Merely by slipping into a fancy dress, a young lady moves into her land of dreams and takes on the identity of her most admired heroine.

But what if the girl who dressed up as Farrah Fawcett-Majors suddenly looked like her? What if the curves my son throws with the dice really made him the best pitcher?

Now we begin to approach a very inadequate parallel to what happens between God and man. Starting at less than a Lab Laz identity level, man is created in the wondrous likeness of God. Not only that, but through faith he is given the privilege of calling God his Father—dressing up like Christ, as it were.

But our lack of resemblance to the Son of God is much more dramatic than the difference between Farrah Fawcett-Majors and the neighborhood's plainest five-year-old girl. Far from being like Christ in uniting our world with that of the Father, we hold on to our greed, our conceit, our self-centeredness. How dare we call ourselves God's children?

The answer is simple. We have been commanded to turn to God as our Father. Otherwise, it would be pointless pretense and unmitigated brazenness to consider ourselves children of God.

Then What Happens?

Dressing up like Christ takes us a step beyond the simple dictates of our conscience. There are many things we think and do that we will have to discard from our lives if we seriously want to resemble Christ. We become less concerned with what we are allowed to do and more concerned with what will bring us into closer conformity with the model we are seeking to imitate. We ask less often, "What's wrong with this thought or action?" and more often, "What's right with it?" We begin to live our lives as if we were painting a portrait rather than following a set of rules.

This is the life-style to which we are called. If we fully understand what is being asked of us, we might be inclined to throw up our hands in a despairing, "No way!" But we need to realize that we are not asked to make this incredible change in ourselves under our own power. The real Son of God is with us, injecting His kinds of thoughts and actions into our beings.

Christ's Loving Assistance

The help we receive became available because the real Son of God has become one of us. He took on the characteristics of our "plastic" humanity—a human body with a specific height and weight, describable facial characteristics, hair of a particular color—everything but sin. In Christ, humanity has one representative who truly is what all humans were intended to be.

We who have been blessed with the Christian faith know where our fulfillment lies, but we continue to fight against it. Much of what is plastic within us does not want to come alive. We find ourselves racing faster and faster in an attempt to outdistance the reach of God's hand. Whenever we hear a word of reproach, we point to the many good things we have done and rationalize most of our unchristian living.

With God's help we can and must turn from this life-style to a life of love. Love in our life shows itself most directly in worship of our Creator. Its secondary expression is through our relationships with fellow human beings.

As we become more faithful to the loving style of life Christ has modeled for us, we will not be content with going through the motions of worship; our worship will be love-filled. We will not be content to treat others charitably; we will truly love them. We will come more and more to resemble the real Son of God in His true humanity.

The infinite richness of God includes a greater abundance of good things for each of us than we can ever possibly imagine. Already He has touched our lives with generous blessing. As we commit ourselves more fully to grow in wisdom and love, the magnificence of God will be revealed to us in ever-widening vision. We will become increasingly conscious of His presence in our lives.

CHAPTER 6

CONSTRAINTS

Whatever you set out to do, something else must be done first.
—Murphy's Sixth Law

Even though I have never known a frog very well, I've always felt sorry for the poor critters because of an experiment I read about. Behavioral scientists are always messing around with animals. They justify what they're doing by pointing out that what they find out is very helpful to man (okay, woman too). Personally, I feel a tinge of sympathy even for Pavlov's salivating dogs on those days when I've just made another resolution to do something about my weight.

In any case, I hope you can use the results of this experiment with frogs to such advantage that it will counterbalance the cruelty with which they croaked—for the last time.

It seems that a number of live frogs were placed in water, which was then heated very slowly. The purpose of the experiment was to discover at what point the frogs would become alarmed at the rising temperature and jump out of the water. The change was so gradual, though, that the poor frogs boiled to death without a protest.

Very gradual changes have a way of conditioning us so that often we are not really aware of what is happening. Unfortunately, our lives sometimes deteriorate in this very slow manner. We become so accustomed to our unfulfilled existence that we don't actually realize how unfulfilled we are.

Perhaps by now, though, you have made up your mind to accept God's promise of a richer life. You have considered what the assurance of God's love and care should mean to you. You have prepared yourself to deal with complications that might arise. You have thought about how you use your money and time and you have assessed your personal commitments. What's next?

The sixth decree from lawman Murphy suggests that you really can't get started. No matter what beginning point you choose, there will always be some constraint to keep you from acting. It's enough to frustrate you to a state of catatonia.

Maybe there's an important do-it-yourself job to be done. Before you can get started you have to retrieve the tools your neighbor borrowed. But you can't locate the tools until the borrower gets home from the bowling lanes, and he can't leave until the guy he's riding with finishes visiting with his friends.

I never seem to have the right tools to do a job. Last Christmas I gave my Hilda what has to be the least romantic gift of all time—two new toilet seats. Obviously, before they could be used they had to be installed. Using my cheap wrenches and a hacksaw (really!) I managed to get one in place. But before the second one was installed I had cracked the toilet bowl, and I had to call five plumbers before I found one that could give same-day service.

Sometimes our imagination creates constraints. Writers, for example, are notorious for imagining things they must do before starting to write. Some have to sharpen every pencil in sight. Some have to clean the typewriter keys before every beginning. Humorist Robert Benchley says he gets important things done by imagining there is some other, more important task confronting him. This enables him to put off the imagined top-priority task, thus taking care of his impulse to procrastinate.

Planning

Another kind of procrastination is taking too long to plan. We try to think through every detail of what we will do, sometimes spending so much time at the drawing board that there is no time left to start construction.

Often a subconscious fear keeps us from getting started. We may be afraid of what might happen or doubt our ability to see the task through. Because some of our past efforts—or efforts of others we know—have not been successful, we put off taking the present risk.

Fear saps our energies. Besides keeping us from making progress, it also confuses us. Worst of all, it undermines our faith.

Christ spoke to this point at the conclusion of the Sermon on the Mount: "Let the day's own trouble be sufficient for the day." He explained what this should mean to us: "Therefore do not be anxious about tomorrow, for tomorrow will be anxious for itself" (Matt. 6:34). Christ was warning us against the most common source of needless anxiety: the imaginary fear of what might be.

This advice was not intended as a counsel to carelessness. Christ was not suggesting that we pay no attention to where we are going or what we need to get there. He was simply advising us to trust God to supply what is beyond our power.

Reliance on God certainly does not mean passivity. We are to choose to do whatever is most in accord with truth and love, concentrating our energies on the present moment. We entrust even the immediate future to God, knowing that the consequences that follow from our actions are sure to be beneficial to ourselves and others. We leave it to God to work out these good consequences in His time, in a manner we can't possibly foresee.

Nevertheless, planning is an inevitable part of our human existence. Because we are limited to experiencing only one moment at a time, we anticipate the future. The decisions we make and the actions we perform are carried out in the context of this anticipated future.

On the other hand, when we talk about *God's* plan, we mean simply that it looks like a plan to us. We're dealing with concepts of God in the only way we can, using finite words and concepts. But our future—like that of all men of all times—is present to God. He has no need to plan.

The same simple perfection that places God above the limits of time also makes His "plan" flawless. Our challenge is to make our planning as consistent as possible with His perfect "plan" for us.

Over the years I have been convinced that planning is a very individual matter. Planning styles differ markedly from one person to another, and we can't even be sure the word means the same thing to different people. Plans vary from a vague sense of direction to a meticulous listing of details. Our psychological needs impel some of us to take great care in thinking ahead, but we should never let our planning for the future cause problems in our present.

We also differ from one another in how we carry out our plans. When I taught university writing courses I used to spend considerable time on the principles of logical outlining. Too often I assumed that once the student had developed a sound outline he would be able to produce a composition that moved in orderly fashion from one part of the structure to another. What I actually found was that the typical student considered the development of the outline plan one assignment and the writing of the composition a completely unrelated task.

Much the same kind of thing happens repeatedly in our every day lives. Carefully developed plans often go for naught. We might draw up very careful plans for a vacation trip only to see a child get sick on the first day. We would go back to the drawing board, but we had to leave that at home along with the swimsuits to make room for all the stuffed animals. (Would you believe that ten of us went to Virginia Beach one summer and not one of us remembered to take swimwear along?)

Need for Flexibility

All this adds up to the need for flexibility. If our plans are too rigid they will be useless and we will be frustrated. Someone has said that the really contented person is one whose yesterdays are filed away, whose present is is in order, and whose tomorrow is subject to instant revision. Humorist Josh Billings said that making firm plans is "like planting toads and expecting to raise toadstools."

If you have decided to make some changes in your life, now is the time to begin. Don't let imagined constraints keep you from getting started. Let yourself begin to move forward now. And when you go swimming and hit the cold water for the first time, remember the frog experiment. Let the suddenness of the temperature change be a reminder that life can be much more satisfying when you aren't afraid to jump in.

Getting Started

In our attempts to move toward a fuller existence, just getting started is often the hardest part. We all need to find means that overcome our basic human inertia.

When we succeed, the rewards are great. "Life leaps like a geyser," says 1912 Nobel prize-winner Alexis Carrel, "for those who drill through the rock of inertia."

To begin now, you might stop reading for a moment and choose a starting point. Try to pin down a specific first action you will take. If possible, commit yourself to this act by telling someone else about it.

One of the hardest things about getting started is that we see so much to be done. Andre Maurois has said, "He who wants to do everything will never do anything." You must set some priorities. Identify some single starting point that is important enough to make it worth the effort.

Many of us live the way we watch television. We might be tuned to a program that is not particularly good, but we don't feel it is bad enough to bother to get up and change it.

We need to recognize that "I must do something" always brings better results than "Something must be done."

Encountering the Unexpected

Two robbers in Salt Lake City did a careful job of planning, but they hadn't counted on the victim's terrified reaction. As they jumped from their hiding place to relieve a twenty-year-old restaurant manager of a $1,700 night deposit, the young man threw up his hands. As he did so the money sack slipped from his clutch, flew through the air, and landed on the roof of the bank.

No matter how you set your sights you are bound to encounter some difficulties or failures. Learning to deal with these negative factors is a big part of maintaining confidence in your ability to succeed.

Your unsuccessful experiences may be little things—

like your attempt to get your child to keep the scissors out of his mouth while he's cutting teeth, or the hungry way the copy machine eats your original documents. Or there may be some chronic problem—like the daily burnt offering some young wives find themselves placing before their husbands.

Whatever your negative experiences, you need to learn to avoid dwelling on them. A quick glance at any of the trouble signs in your life is all it takes to be sufficiently aware of them.

When the red light on the dash of your car comes on to indicate that your battery is not charging, do you pull over to the side of the road and sit staring endlessly at the light? Of course not. As quickly as you can you find your way to a service station and have the problem corrected. This is exactly how you should deal with other trouble signs in your life.

Pass over the difficult moments quickly. Entertainer Carol Channing was once asked by a reporter, "Miss Channing, do you remember the most embarrassing moment of your life?"

"Yes, I certainly do," said Carol. "Next question?"

Keep Moving

Although it's important to get yourself on the right track, you'll get run over if you just sit there. You need to progress steadily toward the goals you set for yourself and you need to be aware of your progress.

The splendid thing about your position is that you are completely free to choose any starting point and any rate of speed you feel comfortable with. If you are inclined to take chances and aspire to a dramatic change in your life, you may do so. Preposterous aspirations sometimes bring extraordinary success. Ludwig Borne says, "True courage is not only a balloon for rising, but also a parachute for falling."

On the other hand, you might be the fainthearted type who is inclined to define confidence as the feeling you have before you know better. Don't be ashamed if you are more comfortable with a less ambitious goal or a slower rate of progress.

After you have made your beginning with all the confidence you can muster, you will need some means of making sure progress continues. Even if you can handle the difficult moments in your life rather well, the enthusiasm with which you begin your task is sure to wane. You will need to discover ways of reviving your positive motivation. This might be nothing more than a review of your goals and priorities as you start off each day. This technique seems to work best for those of us who are fairly alive and fresh at a day's beginning.

Many people, however, are slow to come alive at the beginning of a day. If you find yourself in this category, try to form the habit of taking an inventory at night.

Some people arrange a special time of solitude each day. This is a perfect setup for inventory. Nearly all experts agree that we can think most effectively in solitude. Sometimes a walk in a quiet place provides the best setting for a daily checkup. You will certainly want to get away for a few moments occasionally, for the sake of reflection and refreshment.

Are you a listmaker? Do you often write down the things you have to remember to do? Now you have an item to add to that list every day. Each day you must *do* some richness. Sound strange? I assure you, that's the way it is. Richness, happiness, fullness of life—these are not things that you *acquire*. If you have tried to pursue them, you have found them elusive. It's time to recognize that they are things you *do*. It's time to give yourself permission to start a full, rich life. Add something specific to your daily agenda.

Measuring Progress

Somewhere in the course of each day, then, you will want to make sure you are taking at least a small step toward your goal. It's important that the question you ask is, "What things have I done right?" more often than "How did I goof up today?" You are looking for signs of progress, and it's almost impossible not to discover some every day if you look hard enough.

Your ability to see daily progress will increase considerably if you translate your top-priority goals into very specific terms. Too often we set a goal for ourselves, make a firm resolution that we believe will get us there, and then move forward in a frenzy, lacking adequate direction. Before long we discover what every mother has always known—that it's much easier to conceive than to deliver. We encounter obstacles that are demoralizing or we find that what we thought was forward movement is not getting us any closer to where we want to go.

Try being very specific both in defining what you hope to accomplish each day and in looking at your evidences of success. It frequently pays to ask three important questions related to any goal or resolution:

1. What is it I hope to accomplish?
2. How will I know when I have done it?
3. What procedures will best help me attain this objective?

Perhaps the goal that has top priority in your life is drawing your family more closely together. You need to ask what this means in terms of specific behaviors, their duration, and their frequency. Will you seek to go somewhere with the entire family every week? Will you arrange at least one hour's joint activity every other day? Will you seek to increase each week the total number of hours you spend together?

Clear definition of your goal will help to identify specific means of reaching it. What does "bringing the family closer together" mean to you? It might be establishing a family relationship with equitable division of responsibility, joint decision-making, and open discussion. Whatever the definition, make sure you have some agreement within the family and the specific means of attaining the goal are appropriate.

How successful should you hope to be? Again, there is no pat answer. The biggest danger, though, is that we seek one hundred percent success and consider ourselves failures if we don't reach this. Even at our best, it is usually unwise to commit ourselves to a success level higher than about eighty-five percent. When I was in school, seventy percent achievement was considered adequate to move forward to the next grade. If you are this successful in attaining your specific objectives, you should be able to take considerable pride in the pace of daily movement toward your goal.

Seeing Things Through

You must learn to think often about the things you usually do well. Step back and admire the attractive meal you've cooked, the skirt you've made, the highlights of the successful meeting you've conducted, the well-received suggestion you made. Whenever you do something that makes you feel proud, relish the feeling, dwell on the incident.

We're not at all accustomed to acting this way. Somehow we have the notion that we should make little of our accomplishments. It is important that we actively try to give equal time to the things we do well. If we wait for recognition of our successes to come from others, we are almost always disappointed. If we do get a compliment, it wears off quickly; we may even reject it immediately. If no one notices, we feel resentment. But compliment yourself and the good feeling stays.

This emphasis on positives is related to both physical and mental health. Medical science today is researching more thoroughly than ever the effect of tensions and self-doubt on physical well-being. The health of those who take an optimistic, positive outlook on life is being compared with that of people who spend their existence standing at the complaint counter. Much evidence is being uncovered to prove that the surly bird catches the germ.

Even the most optimistic of us, though, have times when we feel like the unlucky fellow whose ship came in while he was waiting at the bus station. Perhaps our clever comments at a meeting were greeted with a tremendous burst of silence. For a man it may come from the realization that the very hairs of his head are numbered—in single digits yet. For various reasons, we all stumble on some days when we feel like the young child whose waking lament was, "Oh, dear, I've lost my place in my dream."

These difficult days must also be accepted, of course, but with the new day we move forward, buoyed up by recalling the things that have gone right in our lives. I like the kind of reminder provided by the University of North Carolina English instructor who presented his class with this poetic line: "Walk with light!" He noted that the author was Anonymous (you've heard of him?); he had found the elegant quotation on a sign at an intersection.

Let yourself measure up to your own expectations. You may have a chore listed on your agenda that you are tempted to put off even though you know this is the day for doing it. Ask yourself how you will feel if you do put it off. If your answer is that you'll probably be unhappy with your procrastination, dig in and do the job today. Then enjoy the good feeling that comes from this accomplishment. You'll be proud of the fact that you have control over yourself.

Imagining how you will feel as a result of certain decisions can also turn up some surprises. It sometimes happens that doing something other than the items listed on your agenda produces even better feelings. You'll know when to change your agenda if you anticipate your subsequent state of mind.

Remember To Say "Thanks"

I hope you are convinced that we *can* deal with the constraints that threaten to block our path to a better life. With some determination we can find a starting point, lay some tentative plans, and move forward with confidence in God. When we encounter obstacles or suffer frustration, we can be sure that even these contribute somehow to attaining our goal. By building in regular progress checks and emphasizing the gains we make, we can stay with the struggle and see it through.

It is important to realize that the very struggle for improvement is enriching. It is the process, more than the result, that adds fullness to our lives. God doesn't need the intended results of our efforts. To accomplish His purpose of bringing us to eternal fulfillment, however, He does need our effort. As we apply ourselves to doing His will, we are opening ourselves to redemption and transformation.

We need to keep our openness when setbacks come. Our trust in God must be sustained. Continuing trust can best be expressed and fortified by thanking God for everything. Even when our most important plans go for naught, we should remember to say "thanks."

Author Merlin Carothers tells the story of an attorney who had been drafted into the Army during the Vietnam War. When he received orders for the war zone, his wife threatened to kill herself. At great length, Chaplain Carothers persuaded the soldier and his wife to give thanks for what was happening, to be really grateful even though they understood none of what God was doing.

That very day the desolation of the young wife was lifted as she met her long-lost brother, the first blood relative she had known since infancy. And that very day the soldier met a lieutenant he had gone to law school with who managed to get the husband's orders changed from Vietnam to a legal office on the same base.

Sometimes God gives us this kind of dramatic evidence of His love and care. But *always* His love and care are with us, guiding us to our goal. We need to turn ourselves—with all our Murphyish ways—over to Him without reservation.

CHAPTER 7

THEY JUST
DON'T MAKE 'EM
LIKE THEY USED TO

*If you improve or tinker with something long
enough, eventually it will break.*
—Murphy's Seventh Law

They really don't make them like they used to, you know. Whether you're talking about bicycles or jet planes, faucets or light bulbs, modern materials and production methods show dramatic changes from those of decades past.

Some of the changes are improvements. A ten-speed bike gets me to my destination faster than the old one-speed. It also enables me to negotiate some hills that my out-of-shape condition would otherwise prohibit. Thanks to jet propulsion, we travel from one side of the world to another in less time than we would have thought possible years ago. Washerless faucets and frosted light bulbs also have some distinct advantages.

The technology that has enabled us to move forward to these improved provisions is a tribute to man's ingenuity. It demonstrates the greatness God allows us to achieve when we address ourselves to productive work activities.

And yet, Murphy reminds us that our improvements will not last forever. We live in a temporary world. Inevitably, the finest products of our labors eventually reach a breaking point.

In this chapter I want to discuss how this lack of permanence should influence the way we approach our jobs and careers. Whether we are highly trained professionals, skilled craftsmen, or hardworking laborers, we put much time into our jobs. Having the right outlook is important.

Murphy suggests a defeatist outlook. Keep trying to improve something and eventually it will break. You'll end up with a car on which everything makes noise except the horn. The engine won't start and the payments won't stop.

"What model is your car?"

"It's not a model. It's a horrible example!"

Our Fragile World

One problem for my family is broken doorknob assemblies. When the one on our front door wore out, it was quite a shock to me to find that nobody made a replacement that would fit. For a longer time than I like to remember, we lived with masking tape holding back the door latch to keep us from getting locked in our own home. Finally we gave up and took the assembly completely out of the door, relying on a single lock to protect us from intruders. Maybe someday we can replace the door—assuming, of course, that I'm willing to cut one to fit.

It's somewhat comforting to know that the Felixes aren't the only people who have problems like this. Henny Youngman once commented that members of his family used to sing very loudly when they were in the bathtub. It wasn't because everybody was all that happy; it was just that the bathroom door had no lock on it.

Let's look at some of the bylaws lawman Murphy might set down.

- A failure will not appear until after a unit passes final inspection.

- In any set of calculations, the figure that is most obviously correct will be wrong.

- All warranty and guarantee statements become void upon payment of invoice.

- The closer a product is to completion, the greater will be the necessity of making a major change.

- Interchangeable parts never are.

- Any box thrown away before assembly of its contents is sure to contain at least two essential parts.

- The probability of mechanical failure is inversely proportionate to the object's ease of repair or replacement.

Another common occurrence is that the things we produce turn out differently from what we expected. They may be used for purposes we hadn't anticipated. Sometimes they victimize us in Frankensteinian style.

Police in Crownthorne, England, stopped a driver going fifty miles an hour in a thirty-mile zone. The man was understandably chagrined.

"I happen to be a pioneer of radar," he said, identifying himself as Air Vice-Marshall Donald "Pathfinder" Bennet. "I was the first to use it in this country and indeed the world. I don't believe the constable knows how to use it, because if he did I would not be here."

Unfortunately the traffic court decided otherwise, and Pathfinder was fined twenty-four dollars.

Alfred Nobel has given us an example of how to turn such unexpected outcomes around. For people of the twentieth century, "Nobel" and "peace" go together. It wasn't always so.

Nobel was the inventor of dynamite. After the death of his brother in 1864, Nobel opened the newspaper one morning and found his own obituary. In identifying the wrong Nobel, the newspaper described him as a "merchant of death" who had accumulated a fortune from the sale of explosives.

Horrified at the thought that this would be the world's assessment of his achievements, Nobel revised his will that very day. He established the coveted prizes bearing his name which are awarded for the advancement of peace among the human race.

Our Contribution

Even though the things we make and work with do eventually break, each of us can contribute to the advancement of the human race in the work we do. We may see our work as dull or insignificant. We may yearn for the opportunity to accomplish greater things. But if we dedicate ourselves wholeheartedly to the work into which we are led, God's providence will do the rest.

Let me share my experience of how the Holy Spirit works in our occupational lives. As I stepped out my back door one morning I was greeted by a panoramic reflection of God's beauty. A carpet of wildly green grass glistened with the lingering refreshment of the night's heavy rain. The carpeting stretched to the edge of the woods, where the domain of innumerable stately trees begins. Each maple and oak that lines the woods seemed to be spreading its branches in a living expression of gratitude for the nourishing rainfall. The trees reached toward a sky in which faint streaks of white accented the rich blueness.

We had prayed it wouldn't rain on this particular weekend, for this was the day we had invited two hundred guests to our house to celebrate the publication of my first book. There was room in our yard, but crowding two hundred people into our humble home would make Macy's at Christmas seem deserted by comparison. Our own eight children often create the illusion of wall-to-wall kids.

God answered our prayers, of course. He gave an attentive ear to the supplications of our family, our friends, our neighbors, our relatives, and the St. Catharine Prayer Circle. Then He sent us a torrent. Water backed up into our basement, flooded our yard, and thoroughly drenched every available outside seating area. Noah, his two seals, and the Ancient Mariner would have felt very much at home.

You would think I'd be used to it by now. God nearly always answers my prayers like that. Take my writing career. Not long ago any tone-deaf mountain yodeler could have taken it for a song. As a bonus I would have given him a few hundred colorful rejection slips.

My dear, encouraging mother tells me I used to sit for endless hours with crayon or pencil and paper, expressing my thoughts and emotions in various illegible forms. Through the years I had put many, many words on paper and many, many, *many* into prayers for literary success. Finishing high school at sixteen and earning my master's degree in English at twenty-one, I aspired to be a well-known author at a young age. Now at forty-five I had finally published a 158-page book. That's a lifetime average of three and a half pages a year!

God's Best Way

But please don't think I'm ungrateful. I know God's way is best, and I don't need to understand His plan.

God watches over every detail of our occupational

lives. He saw me as I took a job trying to teach English to hundreds of reluctant teen-agers because I couldn't possibly support my wife and child on an income from writing. He saw me moving into school counseling, where I could deal more directly with the personal concerns and values of these young people. He saw me advancing to a position in educational program development and research, where I could further build my writing skills while providing adequate support for my growing family. He saw me moving into the psychology profession in private practice.

All this has been God's will for my life. But if things had gone my way my life would have been very different.

I would have had publishers gobble up those first masterpieces that came from my typewriter and come clamoring for more. I wouldn't have sent a man of my talents into a high-school classroom where a student would threaten me with a knife for taking him to the office. But then I would never have known the comfort of another student's letters across the years:

> When I stop to think of how much I've confided in you, I am shocked! I've never been able to talk to anyone the way I've poured out my heart before you. . . .

> Prayers have gone unanswered for so long that I don't know where to turn next. Never before has my belief in God and His providence seemed so far away. . . .

> God is a lot smarter than we are, and His way is better than ours. Why shouldn't I trust Him? . . .

> I cannot recall a time when I have been so free or so emotionally stable. Realism has taken on a new meaning. I have come to know that we cannot

always do what we would like to do; that restraint is a truly great virtue in many respects. . . . Marriage has done much for me . . . .

Our baby is not an ordinary baby and he is not the kind of baby most people have. Because he is so sick and has so many problems he will need lots of care and help . . . . I feel very lucky that God has given us such a wonderful baby. We love him very, very much and we hope you will love him too.

Yes, I would have done things very differently. Over the years I would have had my typewriter pecking out thousands of pages of salable material. I would have minimized the interruptions of howling infants, jelly-fingered toddlers who jam the typewriter keys, and the amplified roar of hard rock. And I would have missed the countless expressions of young wisdom that have enriched my life:

"On the Fourth of July we thank God because we're all free." "I'm not! I'm four."

"My dad has a mustache, does yours?"
"I'm not sure. If he has one, he keeps it shaved off."

"What does chocolate taste like?"
"It's just the opposite of vanilla."

"I like King Solomon. He was so nice to ladies and animals."
"How do you know that?"
"The Bible says. It says Solomon kept seven hundred wives and three hundred porcupines."

"Does your coach let you play much?"
"No, I'm a pinch hitter and we haven't been in a pinch yet."

LORD, HAVE MURPHY!

Our Need for Trust

And while I was doing things differently, I would have made this special weekend of celebration clear and sunny from beginning to end. I wouldn't have sent the rain on Friday and Saturday—the rain that brought me to the act of resignation: "Dear God, I trust in You completely. Let us have whatever kind of weather You know is best for us."

Then I would have missed the real wonder of this gloriously sunny morning. I would never have experienced the awe of seeing the sun dry the earth especially for our celebration. And I would never have known that finishing touch of the Master as He led me to walk over to the phonograph on the patio, put on a record at random, and feel tears of joyful gratitude welling from deep inside as I heard the first song, "Oh, What a Beautiful Morning!"

God knows we need to trust Him. Acknowledging our complete dependence and confidence is a must for spiritual growth. In our working lives, God very often gives us the opportunity to develop this kind of trust. In one way or another He upsets our sense of security and self-sufficiency and invites us to turn to Him.

It's not good for us to have complete job security. All too soon we become lethargic and uncreative. We fail to exert our best energies because we feel we can get by on less. And we slip into a rut, tending to do things as they have always been done rather than seeking improvement.

Knowing the detrimental effect such conditions can have on humans, God sees to it that periodically our vocational stability is shaken a little. The economy dips and our job tenure is no longer quite the protection it used to be. The duties of our position get shuffled or a new boss who doesn't understand us comes on the scene.

114

Sometimes it's just a matter of being forced to interact with people who see things differently than we do. In my work with the schools several years ago, I was assigned the task of developing a time accounting system for school counselors. The purpose was to analyze the kinds of services counselors were giving to students and see whether these services fit what the students and their parents thought were important. The counselors were not happy at all with the added responsibility of keeping track of what they did all day long. At meeting after meeting their criticism flowed like gushing water, eating away at my pride and temperamental disposition. But I grew.

Dealing with Tension

Experiencing job-related tensions is universal, regardless of the nature of the work or the extent of the responsibilities. We need to recognize these tensions and pressures as opportunities for personal growth. As we do our best to cope with them we should remind ourselves that God will always give us the help we need.

Let me offer five general suggestions for dealing with the pressures that accompany our jobs:

1. Deal with only one problem at a time. Stop letting yourself be overwhelmed by the pressures of having many things to do. It takes only a few minutes to sort out priorities and decide which task to tackle first. And it's so relieving. Remember that jobs are not tense; people are.

2. Use physical activity or constructive recreation to get rid of tensions. Everybody needs a break now and then. If the nature of your job doesn't build in a time to get away, provide this opportunity on your own initiative.

3. Improve the way you treat others. Try to be more tolerant and less critical. Even when you're right, give in occasionally; it's easier on your nerves.

4. Evaluate your general living habits. Make sure you're getting enough sleep and a proper diet. See whether your general life habits are consistent with what you believe in and what you want yourself to be.

5. Talk out your tensions. Sharing your troubles with a friend often relieves tension and puts things in perspective. Be ready to listen when somebody else has a problem, but also give yourself the break of openly discussing things that bother you.

If our work is not going well, we must seek further nourishment to carry it out in a better way. We need to open ourselves and allow the love of God to penetrate more completely. We need to give thanks to God in the midst of our work activity, throwing open the door to our everyday living so He might enter and become an integral part of our occupations.

Something Better?

From time to time, however, discouragement is bound to overtake us. At such times we might wonder whether a job change would be good. One man had worked successfully for fourteen years finding work for handicapped persons. Then the difficulties involved in his work caught up with him and he turned to other occupational areas for satisfaction. But he didn't find it. Finally he went back into the job placement field, saying, "I'm going back. . . . This assignment will be to place workers who have been displaced by automation." His brief experience with other kinds of work had renewed his dedication. God uses our discouragement to accomplish good purposes.

In fact, the Lord often leads us through paths that seem to be circular. We may feel called to one career field, but later find that another seems more suitable. Certainly we should never change impetuously; in fact, it is usually unwise to make a decision to change during a time of unusual discouragement or depression.

On the other hand, we should never cling to a way of life simply because it feels comfortable or gives us a degree of happiness. If there is enough reason to feel that a change is in order, we should make the change without regret. We do not feel sad when we see blossoms falling off the trees. They must go because fruit is coming. In our lives, too, one stage of development passes to another.

Unfortunately, many people today seem to be locked into occupations that bring them little or no satisfaction. Often this happens because people don't take time to study carefully what their true talents and interests are. At other times they may sacrifice work that is interesting or challenging to take a job that offers more financial profit. But to have a job that takes its toll of our time and strength and gives only money in return is a tragic situation.

We need to ask ourselves questions such as these: Does this choice seem to be part of God's plan for my life? Would this job use my talents well? Is it something I am interested in doing? What future opportunities does this position hold? What are my motives for considering this particular job?

Our Partnership

A sense of partnership with God will give us a clearer sense of direction. We need to walk the fine line be-

117

tween sloth and excessive ambition. The slothfulness that is part of every person's nature might tempt us to remain with a job that is easy and unchallenging rather than move forward to one in which our God-given talents could be used more effectively. We aren't necessarily being humble to say, "I'm very satisfied to stay where I am." If a different job would be more fulfilling, we should at least consider the possibility of changing to something better. On the other hand, excessive ambition might impel us to seek greater power or a larger income for its own sake, regardless of how much satisfaction the job might bring or any other indications of God's will.

A University of Michigan survey of 2,500 skilled workers in a large public utility turned up five important factors involved in job satisfaction. These were:

1. *Achievement*—workers need to feel they have done something worthwhile or important.

2. *Recognition*—they need to have their achievements made known to others.

3. *Autonomy*—workers desire a feeling of power over their own actions and areas of responsibility.

4. *Affiliation*—it is important to have friends and to be in communication with others.

5. *Evaluation*—workers need to feel that the standards for judging their behavior and performance are reasonable and just.

Every job should allow the worker to develop his potential. It should never push him down or make him less of a person. Providing an adequate wage is one important factor, but work should also include opportunity for fulfillment through self-giving and acceptance of responsibility.

A Christian view of work sees human beings laboring under God to complete the creative process. Some of us—parents, psychologists, ministers, entertainers, artists —work with souls and minds. Others work with physical materials. Our human methods of measuring results are not necessarily the same as God's. We can't really say that one person's contribution is more important than another's. Unless our work is positively destructive or an obvious waste of energy and time, we can be sure we are doing part of God's work whether we are aware of it or not.

If we recognize that the work we do makes us partners with God, we can find a great deal of joy in even the most cumbersome tasks. We will be more ready to put our best efforts into our jobs, however lowly they might seem. We will be honest and conscientious in our work, giving a full day's effort for a full day's pay, using water cooler and rest area sparingly, and seeking to turn out the best product or render the best service we can.

Evaluating Our Work

The contribution of any one person—even a lifetime of faithful service—will usually seem small. Most of the great products of our efforts and the inventions that have moved mankind forward have been the work of many people working together or one person building on what another has previously accomplished. Our individual work contribution seems relatively insignificant in comparison with the total output of man's efforts or in comparison with God's infinity. But this is not the most meaningful way to assess the value of our labor.

A better kind of evaluation would be based upon the intensity of the love we invest or the purity of our motives. If we put ourselves wholeheartedly into our work, our contribution is almost certainly as valuable in God's eyes as anyone else's. If we realize fully that God in no way needs the results of our efforts, if we drive home the truth that He could instantly erect the world's tallest building as easily as He created the world around it, if we remember that His first and greatest command is love—then we can understand how the assembler who attaches the body of the car to the chassis is truly contributing as much as the medical researcher who discovers a cure for a fatal disease.

We give thanks not only for the stars, the flowers, the moon, and the sea, but also for the things man has transformed from the gifts God has given us. Consider the magnificent universe God has given to man. Think of the seventy-times-seven wonders of the world that we have just begun to discover. With each new marvel man feels he has attained such a height that he can scarcely move beyond it. And yet, always there is more.

We have really just begun to open God's presents to us. Every day man progresses farther, learning to master new realms and putting things to new uses.

Sometimes we make the mistake of thinking of work as a punishment inflicted on man as a consequence of sin. This is not true. Work is actually a great honor conferred on human beings by our Creator. The effect of sin is that work has become a *burden*. We don't enjoy the activity of our work experience as the honor it is. As in other areas, sin has taken away some of our freedom to experience the good things of God's world as they were intended to be.

120

Christ came to add meaning to work as a form of human activity. When we offer our work to Christ, what might otherwise be worthless human activity becomes a means of glorifying God and serving others.

CHAPTER 8

YOU'RE NOT LISTENING TO ME

By making something absolutely clear, somebody will be confused.
—Murphy's Eighth Law

If communication were easy, you wouldn't read so much about it. The eighth law from our pessimistic legislator suggests that all our attempts at clear communication are inevitably doomed to failure.

Recently I read about another piece of legislation—this one known as Gumperson's Law. I was impressed by the fact that Gumperson (I refuse to try to find out who *he* was) seemed to have a better command than Murphy of the kind of language ordinarily used to express laws. Gumperson's Law says: "The contradictory of a welcome probability will assert itself whenever such an eventuality is likely to be most frustrating or, in other words, the outcome of a given desired probability will be inverse to the degree of desirability."

Gumperson's Law would probably cover such well-known facts of life as:

- The worst toothaches always come when your dentist is on vacation.

- Vacant parking spots are always on the other side of the street.

- Grass seed grows better in driveway cracks than on front lawns.

Or consider the following incident that allegedly occurred in a small-town bank. The teller's cage had recently been equipped with a burglar alarm. If the teller pressed the pedal sunk in the floor behind her foot, a bell sounded at police headquarters. Within a few days after installation, a gunman stepped up to the window, demanding the money in the drawer. The girl stepped back on the pedal. After some five seconds of anxious silence, the phone rang and the teller reached for it. But the gunman grabbed it himself, lifted the receiver, and heard an irate voice: "This is the police. Do you know you have your foot on the pedal that rings the alarm down here?"

Confusion is inevitable, Murphy says. And you have seen enough instances of communication failure to appreciate what he means. After hearing a detailed explanation, one puzzled woman said to her lawyer, "Can you explain it in something simpler than 'layman's terms'?"

Human lawmakers are very concerned with making sure the legislation they formulate covers all possible situations. But it can't. One need only consider the frequency of cases in which judicial decisions are reversed by higher courts to realize the ambiguity of applying our laws to real-life situations.

The same problem exists with God's laws. Although the Ten Commandments are very clear and concise, it isn't easy to apply them to everyday living. Sometimes we get mixed signals concerning the right thing to do. We may decide to act conscientiously and follow the will of God, but we often have difficulty determining what He wants.

We don't always receive God's communications clearly. We also have trouble communicating with Him in prayer. Frequently we encounter difficulty in communicating with one another. Let's examine each of these problem areas.

What's That Again, Lord?

To say that God has trouble communicating with us may seem disparaging to His divinity. But the weakness is ours, not His. A pro quarterback might throw his passes very consistently on target, but if the receivers hide behind the defense or keep their hands behind their backs, pass completions won't occur.

Often we are much more ready to receive what we are taught about ancient history or geometry than the truth of the gospel. Why this resistance to Christ's teaching? Some would attribute it to the many mysteries the gospel imposes. But the fact of three persons in the Godhead is not what worries most of us. Rather, it's the gospel's moral code. Christianity demands a manner of conduct in which we see many restraints. Quite naturally, we fear it.

One of our key problems is the pragmatic values and attitudes that permeate our life-styles. A basic Christian view of the real world is lacking. We have given up much of our power to appreciate and understand human dignity, truth, and love. Instead, our lives are guided by confused pragmatic ideas about how things can be used and what course of action is feasible.

We are prisoners of a sense of urgency. Because we have lost our perspective and our sense of values, we can no longer estimate correctly the outcomes of our choices and actions. We may be able to predict that certain things will happen when we behave in a certain way, but we are unable to grasp the significance of these results.

We need to turn this condition inside out. If we can restore our basic Christian outlook and let it permeate our way of life, we will be more able to choose good alternatives and actions in spite of immediate consequences that may be threatening. When we choose what seems good we can be assured that the ultimate consequences will be good.

This does not mean we ignore possible dangers that might result from our choices. Rather, we ask God's guidance and consider the alternatives carefully, trying to be sure that what we choose is consistent with His plan.

Finding God's Will

Christians have devised various ways to determine God's will for their lives. Keith Miller describes a technique attributed to Swiss psychiatrist Paul Tournier. Each morning Dr. and Mrs. Tournier would pray together, asking God what questions He had for them. They would spend about twenty minutes in silence with pencil and paper, writing down questions that came to mind. Then they would share what they had written.

Listening for questions creates a situation in which our daily living seeks to provide answers. The questions will arise out of our subconscious and be based on past experiences. But if we are truly open to God, He will bring forth those questions He wants us to consider.

Herbert J. Taylor has set down what he calls "The Four-Way Test." He recommends that we consider four questions in evaluating God's will in any possible action:

1. Is it the truth?
2. Is it fair to all concerned?
3. Will it build goodwill and better friendships?
4. Will it be beneficial to all concerned?

We also look to the Bible. What does God's written Word tell us to do? Usually it is best to stick with the literal or traditional interpretation of the Bible message and how it applies to our lives. In other words, don't look for between-the-line meanings or search out biblical passages that can be twisted to suit certain preferences.

One day when W.C. Fields, that great motion picture actor, was near death, a friend visited him and found him reading the Bible. The friend was surprised; Fields had never been a religious person.

"Bill," the visitor said, "I'm deeply touched. . . ."

"Don't bother," Fields replied. "I'm just looking for loopholes."

Being honest in seeking guidance from the Bible is related to sincere listening for the Word of God in our hearts. If we honestly attempt to walk with and communicate with the Holy Spirit, if we open our hearts as widely as we possibly can to His guidance, disparity between what the Bible tells us to do and what we hear in our hearts is likely to vanish.

It is very important that we first make ourselves attentive to God's Word and *then* begin to survey the situation. If we begin with our circumstances we waste much effort and needless anxiety on pointless reflection, discussion, and study. We need God's guidance in examining our situation to decide the right course of action.

In each act and choice of our lives we should try to follow the best light we have. We cannot stand around waiting for thorough vision, paralyzed by doubt and uncertainty. If we dare to move forward, even at the risk of making a mistake, God will give us direction. If we do what seems right, we are open for God to give us His inspiration for further action.

In many situations it is extremely difficult not to make a mistake. Our judgment may be blurred by some strong psychological need or by our own closeness to the situation. Sometimes we subconsciously erect detours that keep us from the truth. We place ourselves in a moral predicament reminiscent of this traffic bulletin on a Boston radio station: "The highway commissioner reports that detour signs will be conspicuously placed so that no one will have any trouble getting lost."

We should never be surprised even at our own worst blunders. I have followed the Ten Commandments all my life; I just wish I could catch up with them! We should never permit ourselves to sink into despair and self-pity. Most of our difficulties arise because we lose heart too easily. Then come the complaints and cries of desperation: "What have I done to deserve this?"

In our attempt to serve God we need to relinquish our self-will. We must surrender as much of ourselves as possible to as much of God as we know. In the process of reaching out to God, we open ourselves so He can make His will known to us.

Our Prayers

By lifting our minds and hearts to God in prayer, we are able to take hold of His infinite abundance. Already He has placed at our disposal all the good that we can possibly comprehend and properly use. As our faith and understanding increase, we become more able to appreciate and use a share of God's abundance.

I had an experience the other day that has caused me to appreciate the gift of faith just a bit more. I had been struggling with a very difficult writing assignment, trying to get my ideas organized and stir up courage to tackle the dictation. Finally I reached the point where I had a sense of organization and perspective and was ready to jump in. I stepped out of my office to summon my secretary only to find she had just left on break.

Somehow I have never outgrown the disappointment I feel when reversals like this occur. I didn't want to start another task lest I lose track of the pattern of organization I had worked so hard to achieve. Not knowing exactly what to do, I picked up the phone and dialed the local number for an inspirational message. I heard the telephone ringing and the answering machine come on the line, but there was no message—only the scraping sound of an erased recording.

We sometimes get the same feeling when we pray. Anyone who has ever sincerely tried to make prayer an integral part of life has found it difficult. Even Christ's prayer was interrupted by the tempter. Most of us eventually come to a point where our hearts are asking, "Are you still there, Lord?"

The more we know about prayer as an act of speaking with God, the more difficulties we seem to have with it. We don't hear children complaining about not being able to pray. Adults who treat prayer as a casual or occasional experience don't report a lot of trouble in their attempts to pray. But for those who try to make prayer a regular part of their lives, problems are bound to come.

We need to realize that overcoming these difficulties is an important part of our growing relationship with God. As we move toward more intimate levels of communication we need to grow in our detachment from self and material possessions. God's help will increase our faith, enable us to overcome the difficulties, and move us toward closer communication with Him.

Jesus Christ has promised that the believer will perform works as wondrous as the miracles Christ Himself performed—or even greater. If we give up our feverish hold on the petty things of life and take firm hold of faith in God, there is no limit to what can be accomplished.

We praise God for His tremendous goodness to us and His infinite majesty. This act of praising helps us grow in our understanding of spiritual truth. It increases our ability to accept God in a larger way. Gradually we expand our consciousness of His presence until it per meates our entire lives with beauty and radiance. Praise develops our inner powers of discernment. It enables us to appreciate more completely the blessings He has prepared for us from the foundation of the world.

Expressing Our Needs

Praise and thanksgiving are the highest forms of prayer. But God also wants us to come before Him with contrite hearts to tell Him of our needs. The trouble is that some of us never get down on our knees until we haven't a leg to stand on.

When we take our problems to God, we must avoid telling Him how He should work them out. We must place no limits on God as to the manner in which He answers our prayers. Rather, we must trust the perfect wisdom of His way. God has ways of taking care of our needs that we have not begun to think of.

Too often we are like a rooster who thinks his crowing makes the sun rise. We fail to acknowledge that God's light brings us to prayer in the first place.

We need to realize that the purpose of prayer is not to change God's mind or to persuade Him to do something for our benefit that He is not in the habit of doing for others. Rather, prayer changes us so that we might be able to receive and use what God has already provided for us. We pray that our consciousness and awareness may be enlarged and our worthwhile activities increased so that we do God's will and work in harmony with the good He has already created for us. We pray so that we might recognize a bit more of God's perfect kingdom in our lives. This kingdom is already in our midst, but it is the kingdom of His Spirit. Prayer is our means of seeing this kingdom.

Expressing our prayers as demands or imperative requests would be an insult to God if we truly realized what we were doing. It's like saying, "Let me tell You something, Lord. I know what has to happen in my life. I reminded You of it before, but at Your age I know You can be forgetful. Now let me have this thing I'm asking for so I can be sure You're out there listening to me."

Change it. Let your prayer come from a humble heart that realizes God always wants to give, but we are not always ready to receive. Say, "Lord, Your grace is always with us guiding us in the way that is best. I want to realize this more completely and be open to all the good things You are sending into my life. Sometimes my weak understanding makes it difficult for me to see that Your way is the best way. I will try to trust You, my loving Lord, and be ready to respond positively to every challenge and opportunity You send me. I adore You as my supreme Lord; I thank You for all the blessings You give. I am sorry for ever doubting You."

Seek to give God a free hand to help you in His own wise and loving way. Erase all doubts and fears from your mind as to how your prayer will be answered. Simply have faith that God, who is wise, infinite, and powerful, will indeed supply an answer. Put your needs confidently into His hands. Plunge actively into His service and leave the rest to Him without worry.

Communicating with One Another

Just as we have difficulty hearing God and expressing ourselves to Him, so also we encounter numerous problems in communicating with one another.

An eighteen-year-old in San Francisco told a ticket agent that she had a hot car. Her boiling radiator didn't really call for the police investigation that followed.

A wife asked her husband, "What makes the stock market go up and down?"

"Inflationary pressures and fiscal instability, ' he answered. "Not to mention international imbalance and political tensions."

After a moment's reflection the wife said, "If you don't know, dear, why don't you just say so?"

And finally there was the woman farmer who wrote to the Department of Agriculture to ask for advice about her chickens. "Every morning for a week I have found a few of my hens lying on their backs with their feet in the air. Can you tell me the reason?"

After waiting a considerable time for a reply, she received an official-looking communication from the department. Eagerly she opened the letter and read, "Your hens are dead."

Despite our difficulties, communication is very important. Since we are to communicate to others whatever good we possess, we need to be concerned with how this communication can take place.

To improve our communication we need to give one another opportunity to explain what is really meant. Our language is sometimes baffling. Goods carried by ship are cargo; goods carried by rail car are shipments.

Most words in our language have more than one meaning. "Glasses" may refer to an implement used to improve our vision; however, if filled with strong refreshment and then emptied, "glasses" may help to seriously interfere with our vision. To a child, "fix" is what his father does to toys. To an adult, the same word refers to a dreaded necessity of life or a severe problem situation. The drug user attaches to it still another meaning.

In the same way, "faith" may have different meanings to different people. To some it may mean the particular framework of beliefs to which they have committed themselves. For others, "faith" may refer to daily living as a means of leading others to God. Some people use faith as synonymous with trust.

As we come to understand better what important words like this means to one another, we should be able to recognize that our different interpretations need not be stumbling blocks to mutual understanding.

Now Listen, Hear

Many of us are very generous with our advice. We feel that our religious beliefs give us answers to many of the questions that haunt unbelievers. We are eager to share our beliefs and insights with them, and sometimes we think this is all it will take to solve their problems.

Unfortunately, giving a map to a traveler doesn't automatically bring him to his destination. If a person is to drive from one place to another, he must first start his engine. He will probably want to look at the map at least long enough to get an idea of what kind of journey lies ahead. If his trip requires him to leave behind a number of prized possessions, he may decide he doesn't really want to go.

Because our journey presents a parallel situation, we often benefit from human help. If someone is willing to listen carefully to us, help us sort through our conflicting values, and respect the points of view we express, we can often bring ourselves to proceed on very difficult—perhaps costly—routes.

We need to listen long and attentively if we really want to understand other people. If we are to help others open their hearts, we must give them time. We must be patient. It is important that we ask only a few questions, and phrase these as carefully as possible, in order to help others explain their experiences. If we are critical or give the impression that we know best, we will put others off and offend their sensitivities. Rather, we need to create a climate of warm, confidential listening and caring.

As we bring ourselves to more genuine caring, we find others increasingly ready to open themselves to us.

133

Our conversation tends to change gradually from surface talk about the weather or sporting events to deeper human concerns.

The technique of "active listening" advanced by psychotherapist Carl Rogers is very helpful. Anyone can learn the basic principles of this technique in a few minutes. Practicing it effectively may take some time. This approach calls for listening for the feelings that underlie verbal expressions, reflecting them back to the person verbalizing them, and showing acceptance of these feelings.

Perhaps a friend approaches you with, "This sure is a messed-up world!"

You reply, "You sound angry and frustrated."

Notice that this first comment goes immediately to the feelings, not the idea content, being expressed. By this reply your friend will be encouraged to pursue his feelings further and talk about them. As you show him that you can accept these as legitimate, he may be helped to see his emotional reactions more objectively and to feel better about his world and his place in it. Someone has defined a friend as one who sees through you and still enjoys the show.

Any time we help another person advance in self-understanding we are advancing God's kingdom. In this area, as in other aspects of human growth, any progress is noteworthy. Helping someone move a little closer to the joy that comes with being in touch with one's self is a very worthwhile contribution. The grave danger is that people might miss all opportunities to grow in self-understanding. We must be careful not to contribute to this tragedy through manipulation, overpossessiveness, or other forms of control.

Taking time to listen and respecting the freedom of others are important ways of avoiding the communication failures predicted by Murphy's eighth law. As we communicate more effectively, we will understand one another better and be mutually supportive in our search for God's will.

Self-Understanding

Our communication efforts also help us to know ourselves better. Relationships with others provide a mirror in which we can see all that we are. Our thoughts, feelings, motives, appetites, fears, and urges are all observable there if we but look at them. We won't see ourselves as we wish to be, just as we are not guaranteed a reflection of beauty when we look into a mirror. What comes back to us is sometimes ugly, and this is why we turn away and refuse to look.

We may see that to those who are able to give us something we are generally very polite, whereas we act rudely or contemptuously to those who demand something of us. We may see false respect, arrogance, and selfishness reflected in our dealings with other people.

Painful as it may be, it pays to study our reflection and seek to know what we really are. As soon as we begin to know ourselves better, we set in motion an unusual process of creativeness. Seeing what we are is an astonishing revelation. It opens us to an ever-deeper understanding of the world around us and the God who created us. Educated people who don't know themselves are actually unintelligent. In self-knowledge we find the door to a richer understanding of all things.

Each of us has a false self that casts a shadow over what we really are. This illusion is the person we want ourselves to be, but who cannot exist because God didn't create him. Our unreal selves want to exist beyond the radius of God's providence. The self that God wants us to be is what we are at any moment when we truly open ourselves to His will.

Unfortunately, we don't recognize our illusions. This is especially true of the unreal self that exists only in our self-centered desires. We try to structure our entire universe around this false self. We spend our time and energies accumulating pleasures, honors, and luxuries to build this illusion into something real. But the product is hollow nothingness. When the transitory dressings have been stripped away, there will be nothing left but a specter that tragically announces we are a mistake.

We find our greatest freedom in humble acceptance of what we are. A little girl was playing in the sand alone. A neighbor called over the fence, "Where's your mother?"

"She's asleep."

"Where's your little brother?"

"He's asleep, too."

Asked the neighbor, "Aren't you lonesome, playing all by yourself?"

"No," said the little girl. "I like me."

If we open ourselves to recognizing our limitations and imperfections without a need to deny or rationalize them, we have begun our move toward liberation. We will be freed of constant focus on our own concerns, worry about what others may think of us, and regret of mistakes we have made.

On the other hand, as long as we feel obliged to defend our vulnerabilities, we are slaves to our ideal selves. To protect ourselves we seek to find fault with others, to criticize them, and to redirect the finger of blame. Many persons sincerely striving to live good lives have become bitter and unhappy because of an unconscious belief that their happiness depended on being more virtuous than other people.

When we are delivered from attachment to our own reputation and goodness, we find we can realize true joy only by completely forgetting ourselves. When we no longer have to pay attention to our own lives, reputation, and excellence, then we become free to serve God for His sake alone.

Listen to Yourself

Take time to listen to yourself. Allow your everyday creativity to go through a thorough processing.

Did you ever come off a particularly hectic schedule and try to slow down suddenly? It's peculiar. You sit down and try to quietly compose yourself, but you find that your heart keeps pounding and thoughts keep whirling through your mind. You slow your body down, but you can't lessen the pace of your imagination. In fact new thoughts—weird ones—seem to come on faster than ever. You may receive new revelations and insights into who and what you really are.

But you have to be ready to face it. You have to be willing to acknowledge that these thoughts and fantasies come from deep within you, from the kind of person who is really you. Nobody else produces your fantasies. The fantasies are part of your nature, part of you.

It's a risky business. You are likely to find out something about yourself that you would really rather not know. You would rather not think of yourself as an adulterer, but there you are in your fantasy running off for a wild weekend with somebody who doesn't really look like your wife. Or you may confront some fear you have long been unwilling to admit. You may wake up in a cold sweat and realize there is something you feel guilty about that you just haven't wanted to face.

The persons we get to know at times like these are the persons that have been formed by our past actions, decisions, and choices. But they are not persons that we have to go on being. With God's help we can improve the kind of people we are.

137

Advancing in self-knowledge and self-acceptance is a prerequisite to growing in our openness to others. Once we have begun to lay aside our habit of hiding behind Murphy, we can more readily acknowledge our own responsibilities, confess our shortcomings, and love ourselves in spite of them. Then, because we are more secure about ourselves, we can more easily turn outside ourselves and begin to share more fully with others. Our hearts will be more open and so will our senses. We will hear the things others say with greater awareness, and our hearts will be more able to reach out to them with sincere concern.

CHAPTER 9

CAN ANYONE BE TRUSTED?

You can fool some of the people all of the time, and all of the people some of the time, and that's sufficient.

—Murphy's Ninth Law

And so we come to Murphy's ninth law and our last chapter. If you've stayed with me this long, you've shown considerable patience. I appreciate that.

But wouldn't you be foolish to believe everything you have read in this book? Undoubtedly, some of what I have written just doesn't ring true. Some of the generalizations I have made on the basis of my limited experience don't fit into the gestalt of your life.

And it's that way with everything we read. We have grown accustomed to news reporters who over-dramatize the day's events. We are used to magazine writers who supply data and other factual material to support their opinions but seldom deal with opposite points of view. And we have read enough biased books that we just aren't ready to give full credence to what any author writes.

This is good. There is only one Book that warrants our full, wholehearted acceptance of all its contents. The Bible sets forth the inspired Word of God and provides a standard of truth against which all other writers can be evaluated. Questioning the other things we read and judging their validity by how consistent they are with the Bible will keep us from being led unwittingly into serious error.

But it is possible to become too skeptical. Murphy's ninth law cautions us to be constantly on our guard. Consider these expressions of unwillingness to trust other people:

"Watch out for the girl who runs her fingers through your hair. She's probably after your scalp."

"You can't trust a guy who comes up and slaps you on the back. He's expecting you to cough up something."

"I found out I can't trust my psychiatrist. First he told me he didn't believe in shock therapy. Then he gave me his bill."

Sometimes it's painful to find out whom you can trust. How often have you put your confidence in a person you considered your friend only to meet with betrayal? How often have you trusted someone to lead you while you obediently followed, only to end up in a blind alley? In a dark theater a young lady was heard saying, "It was bad enough that he lied to me about his yacht. But then he made me row yet!"

Wanting to Trust

It's a natural human quest to try to find somebody we can trust. Still, we learn from the School of Hard Knocks that it is far safer to protect ourselves from pain by not trusting others. This fear of being hurt makes us defensive and insecure. It can be overcome only through the ability to love. We need to progress to the point where we are willing to risk being betrayed to give ourselves in trust to another.

Trusting takes many forms. It can be taking the risk of giving attention to a person in trouble when our natural inclination would call for a more self-centered form of activity. It can be remaining supportive of another even when that person betrays us. It can be accepting the word of another and staking some part of our own welfare on the truth of that word.

Someone once asked Mrs. Einstein whether she understood the theory of relativity. "No," she replied, "but I know my husband and I know he can be trusted."

Trust changes people's lives and enables them to grow. Trust is dynamic, not fixed and unchanging. It can be lost, taken back, and given anew. When trust is freely given without regard for the cost, it has power of profound influence on the lives of those who receive it.

It is impossible to successfully pretend trust. The imitation is detected almost immediately by almost every person. When we are trusted we are aware of it, and we should also be able to recognize times when we are challenged to trust others. The distinguishing characteristic of Christian trust is the ongoing support and concern we offer to others as we keep ourselves available to them.

One of the hardest things Christians are asked to do is to be concerned sincerely with others more than with themselves. We are by nature compelled to be most concerned about self and to be free to look to others' needs only when our own have been met. The press for self-preservation is constant.

With this kind of makeup it is humanly impossible to give completely of ourselves for the welfare of others. Only with the support of God's love can we truly move toward unselfish giving. We need to put down our defenses of our own rights and open ourselves as completely as possible to exclusive concern for fellow man.

We won't do this perfectly. Even with God's help we will lapse into our selfish patterns. But we can't afford to be discouraged. With each failure, we pick up and begin anew, redeclaring our willingness to present our bodies as living sacrifices.

In Whom Do We Trust?

We give of ourselves with as little concern as possible for our own well-being. Although we recognize the possibility of betrayal, we are confident that God's love insures our ultimate safety. We trust God, and because we do we attempt to develop trust toward our fellow human beings.

If we worry instead of trusting, it is a sign that we need more faith in God's goodness and love. When things don't go well, this is very difficult. We all have days when we feel like the seven-year-old girl who was sent home from a birthday party because she got into a fight. When she arrived home, she learned that her cat had been run over. This was too much for her, and she cried tearfully, "This is the worst day I've ever been to!"

"Adversity is what makes you mature," says Charlie Brown in one of my favorite Peanuts cartoons. "The growing soul is watered best with tears of sadness."

Lucy gives him a quizzical look. "What?" she asks.

Charlie starts to repeat his statement, but then says resignedly, "Oh, forget it. . . . I could never say something like that twice in one day!"

In leading us heavenward, God lets no event or trivial incident in our lives escape His notice. Everything that happens to us He wills or permits for a reason. His love for us and His ability to provide are infinite. What greater basis for trust could we hope for?

Trust provides a God-given peace of mind in which we confidently expect God to keep His promise of eternal salvation and the things we need to reach this goal. Just as God cannot deceive us in what He teaches, so He cannot let us down when He promises an eternal destiny. If we seek the kingdom and the justice of God, everything else will be given to us.

CAN ANYONE BE TRUSTED?

Following the Shepherd

Christ is our shepherd. He has told us His loving care will lead us home. In His care we are totally safe. Although the night is dark and we wander far from home, we have complete reason for trust and confidence. We know He will bring us home safely.

Too often we act like little Jimmy, who was standing on the corner when the minister asked him how to find the post office. The boy led him the several blocks to his destination.

"That was certainly kind of you," the minister said. "Would you like to come and listen to my sermon this evening? My topic is 'The Way to Heaven.'"

"Heck," said Jimmy. "you didn't even know the way to the post office."

Sometimes the path to our goals will be blocked. When we find ourselves blocked on one road in life we can always turn to another that will open to us. And the amazing discovery that waits for us on this apparent detour is that the road God routes us on is invariably much more direct than the one we chose in the first place.

Whatever road God's loving care has put us on, we should be grateful. It does everything any road was ever meant to do; it leads us home. Sometimes our paths seem to lead to blind alleys, but we know these will open to brilliant vistas of glory. We know, too, that the steep and difficult terrain over which the Lord guides us will take us to that homeland where every yearning of our hearts will be fulfilled.

But our trust in God goes much farther than simply looking forward to the great homecoming. True, if we are faithful followers we will reap the rewards of a blessed eternity that far exceeds everything we can imagine. But our hope extends to a confidence in God's

143

power to straighten out our bungled lives even now while we are still on this earth. We look to God on a day-to-day basis. In the Lord's Prayer, "thy kingdom come" expresses our long-distance hope while "Give us this day our daily bread" expresses our immediate hope.

I also like the prayer of Bobby Richardson, former second baseman for the New York Yankees, at a meeting of the Fellowship of Christian Athletes: "Dear God, Your will—nothing more, nothing less, nothing else. Amen."

When Things Go Wrong

Today was one of those days when everything goes wrong—at least it seemed that way for the first eleven hours.

I started by oversleeping. Getting up late costs me some of the most precious time of my day, the time I ordinarily devote to special projects. Perhaps the mood this stirs up in me is partially to blame for what happens as the day goes on.

Next, one of our kids—the one who's preparing for a career in dawdling—was extra slow in getting out the door and caused some of our school-age kids to miss the bus. I chased after it for a couple of miles and finally headed it off by going straight in a left-turn-only lane. I assume the kids got to school all right, but by that time the pattern of my morning had been well established.

One after another, things kept going awry. Each small event seemed more out of proportion than the one that preceded it. Such succession of frustrating circumstances has a way of bringing out the worst in me. By eleven I was extremely on edge, ready to clobber anyone who came between me and my selfish goals. I struggled to hold on to some thread of trust that all this nonsense was happening for a purpose.

Suddenly, within about two minutes, four things happened to bring some of my efforts to success. A problem I had been struggling with for some time was suddenly resolved. A person I had been trying to contact by phone to change an appointment called me because of a conflict he had. Another confusing situation was suddenly brought into the light, and a person I had been looking for in the office walked in right at that same moment.

Finally, as one small reminder that the Lord still occupies His throne, I was given the realization that I could grab the dictaphone, make a record of this hectic morning, and make up for the disappointment that had started my day.

The Reality of Providence

We often act as if the providence of God is something new in our beliefs. What really happens, I think, is that our faith deepens with each full experience we have in witnessing God's sovereign hand at work in our lives. God knows we need reminders. We know that if we give our lives to the pursuit of the kingdom of God, nothing else should worry us. And yet we find it very difficult truly to take God at His word and to act as if we expect Him to keep His pledge. We do worry about things; our Lord's promise does not have the impact on our minds that it should have.

God's love toward His children sometimes seems more real if we compare it to human family relationships. It doesn't happen often any more, but occasionally we do still have a precious time when our entire family sits down to a meal together. Since my oldest son has struck out for his own independence, there's almost always somebody missing. When he happens to come around for a meal, one of our other young adults is usually out on a job or some social undertaking.

Last Christmas morning, though, we did all gather together for breakfast. I can't remember when sausage and eggs ever tasted so good.

On these special occasions I get a warm feeling of satisfaction from knowing I have succeeded in providing for this family of ours. I look around the table and watch them giving nutrition to the healthy bodies they have been blessed with. I admire the strong physical frames of my sons (the ease with which most of them can defeat me in arm wrestling gives me fair warning of what would happen if we ever seriously tangled!). I admire the delicate strength of my two daughters and thank God for the joy their wholehearted femininity has brought to my life.

I would do anything for them, of course. I would go anywhere and bear any burden to provide for their needs. I would starve rather than see them go hungry.

Throughout their young years, neighborhood bullies would pick on them. I would become very angry and want to deal with the aggressors myself. Sometimes the attack would come from a person who had been angered by something my wife or I had said or done. Because the bully was unable to strike back at the responsible adult he would take it out on our children. This cowardly behavior was infuriating.

God is a loving Father who wants always to care for us and protect us. He will go anywhere and do anything to show His love for us. The extremes He will resort to are best shown in His redeeming act of coming to our earth. He took on Himself the humble condition of humanity and died a criminal's death so we might have everlasting life.

The devil is a cowardly bully who is eternally angry because of what God has done. Lacking the guts to take on God Himself, the devil picks on His children. He attempts to lead us into acts and decisions that will bring us grief and suffering.

Where Are You, Lord?

When we see the devil succeeding it makes us want to cry out to the Lord and ask Him to stand up and be seen. Why does God usually work so quietly and unobtrusively? Why doesn't He move out of His hiding place and let the cunning, cocky criminals of the world see Him as He really is? We want Him to move in forcefully and take the Murphyish misery out of our lives.

We are sure that if Jesus showed Himself to today's world as He did two thousand years ago, things would be very different. The modern world is rejecting Christ without really knowing Him. We want people to see the real Christ of compelling power and raw muscle. We want them to know the toughness of the skin that withstood the cruel torture that preceded Calvary, the strength of the body that housed so sensitive a spirit.

We know that this Christ will eventually be seen. He will come again with great power and majesty! He delays because He wants to give us an opportunity to choose Him freely. The choice is ours—now.

The play will be over when the Author walks onto the stage. Then we will have no more choice. When the Lord appears without disguise, the natural world will fade like a dream and we will discover the never-ending destiny we have chosen for ourselves in accepting God's way or insisting on our own. Now is our chance to choose. Christ is holding back to give us that chance, but it won't last forever.

Our Choices

A mother told her child: "Look, I don't mind you bringing in turtles and toads. I said you could have hamsters as long as you take care of them. But I can't tolerate snakes. There's just not room enough in this house for both me and a snake. One of us has to go. Take your choice.''

To the mother's consternation, the child took considerable time to ponder his choices. Finally he said, "Oh, all right," and headed for the woods, snake in hand.

But what a shock it was to realize that her son could actually consider choosing the snake over her! At that moment she realized what it must be like for God when man sins.

God reached out to us to extend an invitation for us to share in the light of His divinity. Man refused His gift of love. In every sin we have committed, in every act of placing our own will above His, we adopt an attitude of refusal. And how does God respond? He presses His love upon us more persuasively. He comes farther in search of us.

The life of a sinner is our life. We move forward a little, overcoming perhaps a small vice or cultivating some positive habit only to find that we have shut God out in some other area of our living. Thus it is that each of us can present himself to God and be eligible for His miraculous forgiveness.

Of one thing we can be sure. God will not give up. He will continue to send into our lives unpredictable events, unprecedented storms, unseasonal climates, and many other situations that have the power to open our eyes.

When I Fall

Because God is a loving Father, He often disciplines me. I make numerous mistakes, doing things that are not good for me or for my fellow human beings. Like a stubborn child I insist on doing what I want instead of what God wants. I often talk myself into believing that what I am doing is right even though I have the feeling deep down that tells me it isn't really so. But I go ahead because I am a weak and sinful human being.

Then God strikes me. He hits me hard enough to get my attention and to make me look honestly at myself and my relationship to Him. He lets me see how imperfect I am and how perfect He is. Sometimes he disciplines me severely, and I complain about it. Sometimes I cry. But then God lifts me, wipes away my tears, and sets me off with a new start.

Learning to fall forward is one of the great lessons of our lives. None of us is ever exempt from the pain of falling. We set goals for ourselves and start out in earnest to achieve them, but soon find we are not quite up to what we aspire to. We make a resolution to avoid some evil act or break some habit we have been enslaved to. We may do well for awhile, but then a stronger temptation comes along and we succumb.

These times of falling often result in falling behind. "Falling on our behinds" might put it a bit more aptly. When we don't attain the goal we have set we are inclined to toss our good objectives aside and resign ourselves to halfhearted living for awhile. Or we may decide our habits are more powerful than we are and give in to subjection.

But there is an alternative. We can learn to fall forward. Falling forward is making use of our falls to continue our progress. If we break a resolution we can admit our weakness and seek forgiveness, recognize the causes of our lapse, and ask God for help in continuing our progress. Never does a fall have to mean giving up.

The Focus

If I am to benefit from Christ's suffering, He must become a very personal friend. His sufferings must become increasingly real to me. Most people are somewhat disturbed when they hear a story of human suffering or misery. Generally, though, the most severe hardships endured by people we do not know will mean very little in comparison to even a slight injury or pain of someone we love deeply. The impact of Christ's sufferings on my life depends considerably on what He means to me, on how close and dear He is. If He is merely a great historical person or a distant authority figure, His sufferings will not begin to mean what they should to me. I will continue being far more concerned about the little things that happen to hurt me or my loved ones.

On the other hand, if Christ is indeed the love of my life, His cross will be the focal point that keeps my spiritual growth intact. It will bring an overflow of courage, strength, and endurance as I face the hardships of everyday living. I will be able to accept the things that happen. Even if the death of a loved one darkens my life, I will accept it as part of His plan. Christ's life was expendable; all other human lives surely must be so. But what is expended is not wasted. There was no futility in Christ's death. So also each of the sorrows that comes into my life has a purpose.

The Cross sets before us a clear mixture of good and evil. Here we see that life and death, pain and joy, belong together. He is Victim and Victor! And in Christ's victory over sin and death, we find the evil conquered by the good, the pain conquered by the joy.

This same Cross gives meaning to the mixture of happiness and suffering in our everyday lives. Perhaps you are in love with someone and your love lifts you up with joy, but at the same time you feel an aching because you cannot love adequately. Or perhaps you move through some great tragedy in your life to a new-found joy and realize the reality of the Easter that always follows Good Friday. As the pain and joy of life are woven together, we find that life's fabric is sturdy and very beautiful.

We can view the circle of the universe as held together by two beams, a vertical one and a horizontal one, forming the shape of a cross. The Cross is in the center of the circle, and from that Christ draws us to Himself. He draws us closer through all the experiences of life—through the death of a loved one, the birth of a child, the song of a bird, the rising and setting of the sun. He draws us into Himself and brings us to a joyful day when we will partake of His resurrection—glorious with Him for eternity.

Although it has been said countless times, the truth seldom penetrates deeply enough: Christ's Easter triumph could not have happened except for the tragedy of Good Friday. Since man's original fall, it has been and always will be impossible to know the glory of victory without first experiencing some form of defeat. When we come fully to accept this fact in the context of God's divine providence, every event of our lives takes on a new perspective. In the suffering of broken or strained relationships, we can know the possibility of an Easter of reconciliation. In the sorrow of lost possessions or departed loved ones, we can be confident of a resurrection of new richness. Easter enables us to gather up all the hurts and agonies of yesterday and use them to enlarge and enrich our lives today.

The Promise of a New Dawn

I wonder whether I will ever drive into a sunrise again without remembering that early summer morning. As is my custom, I had been up and working before dawn. The telephone rang and I answered it quickly before it aroused other family members. My niece was calling to give me the sad news that my father had just died.

I woke my wife and, as quickly as we could, we got into the car to travel the several miles to the house I grew up in. I remember the doubt that wanted to hold on in my mind. Had I really heard my niece correctly through her tears? Maybe she had said something like, "Grandpa might die"? But as I headed east into the dawn, I knew. Dad's long-awaited dawning had come. I felt his influence beckoning me to continue to follow in the path he had shown me until we would be together again. I felt a togetherness at that moment like I had not known since the days of my early childhood.

There was a promise in that new dawn. Through the pain of my loss, I knew the joyful anticipation of blissful reunion. I experienced fullhearted trust that this sad experience, like all others in my life, would have a good effect.

I hope this book has increased your awareness of the promise of a new dawn. I hope you realize more fully that Murphy's Laws, although they may be legitimate expressions of our human perplexities, are always superseded by God's promise that He is with us. We can trust Him to keep His Word. It's a fact: All things *do* work together for good for those who love Him.

God's hand is at work in the unexpected complications that confront us in the routine of everyday living. His loving Spirit is completely in control as we struggle to find enough money and enough time to carry out the duties of our lives. God sees us through the risks we take in making commitments. He helps us overcome the constraints that get in the way of accomplishing our goals. His guiding hand is available to us in the work we do and in our attempts to reach out to Him and those around us.

We can trust Him completely.